# OPPORTU~~NITIES~~

# Electronics Careers

Discarded by
Santa Maria Library

SANTA MARIA PUBLIC LIBRARY  06/08

D0401573

# OPPORTUNITIES

in

# Electronics
# Careers

## REVISED EDITION

**MARK ROWH**

New York   Chicago   San Francisco   Lisbon   London   Madrid   Mexico City
Milan   New Delhi   San Juan   Seoul   Singapore   Sydney   Toronto

The McGraw-Hill Companies

**Library of Congress Cataloging-in-Publication Data**

Rowh, Mark.
Opportunities in electronics careers / Mark Rowh. — Rev. ed.
p. cm.
ISBN 0-07-147607-5 (alk. paper)
1. Electronics—Vocational guidance. I. Title. II. Title: Electronics careers.

TK7845.R68 2007
621.381023—dc22 2006028899

Copyright © 2007 by The McGraw-Hill Companies, Inc. All rights reserved. Printed in the United States of America. Except as permitted under the United States Copyright Act of 1976, no part of this publication may be reproduced or distributed in any form or by any means, or stored in a database or retrieval system, without the prior written permission of the publisher.

1 2 3 4 5 6 7 8 9 10 11 12 13 14 15 16 17 18 19 DOC/DOC 1 0 9 8 7

ISBN-13: 978-0-07-147607-2
ISBN-10: 0-07-147607-5

Interior design by Rattray Design

McGraw-Hill books are available at special quantity discounts to use as premiums and sales promotions, or for use in corporate training programs. For more information, please write to the Director of Special Sales, Professional Publishing, McGraw-Hill, Two Penn Plaza, New York, NY 10121-2298. Or contact your local bookstore.

This book is printed on acid-free paper.

This book is dedicated to my friends Bill Burns and Jim O'Hara and to technical wizards everywhere.

# CONTENTS

Electronics versus electricity. Development of
electronics. Advantages of a career in electronics.
Reviewing options.

Career possibilities. Repair and installation of home
entertainment equipment. Repair of commercial and
industrial electronic equipment. Electronics
engineering and engineering technology. Specialized
electronics areas. Job titles. Background and skills
needed. Future prospects.

# Foreword

When seeking a skill or profession to learn in order to get a job, it's a good idea to look for one in which we can make money and find challenge. Otherwise we might just as well play computer games or wait for our parents or the government to feed and clothe us. Most of us do learn the basics like reading, writing, and arithmetic, and some are fortunate enough to receive training in technical school that can prepare us to step right into a rewarding job. Thousands of electronics technicians do that each year and find a career where the universe is the limit.

Some jobs are so interesting and enjoyable that you are eager to leave for the workplace in the morning and not in a hurry to leave work in the evening. Most people do not have such a job. Most people count the minutes and seconds until quitting time so that they can go home or to the bowling alley or some other place of entertainment, because the job is not interesting. If it were not for the paycheck, they would not want to be there.

Few jobs that electronics technicians do are boring. Most are so important that the excitement lingers throughout the career. Technicians keep the high-tech world turning. The interstates and freeways must have technicians to keep their communications systems working; airliners could not take off or land without avionics navigation and computer controls; the world of entertainment, with satellite TV, data, and radio, relies on electronics technicians to maintain the sophisticated systems. Today's smart-house and residential electronics systems would be mind-boggling to someone from the 1950s. Space technology and exploration depend on electronics communications and telemetry such as we could only dream of about fifty years ago. Technicians know how it all works and they make it all work.

A professional technician is not required to be an expert in all areas of electronics. Most are expert in several related areas. But to be in a profession where, if you desire, you can expand your knowledge and skills ever further, is a plus most crafts or professions do not have.

Another advantage for electronics technicians is that they know how things work. Most people who use palm pilots, DVDs, memory sticks, money machines, cell phones, plasma TV displays, and Internet resources haven't any concept of how these products work. Technicians do. In fact, many technicians eventually become interested in astronomy, where the mysteries of magnetism and gravity are so closely related to electronic circuit theory. On the other end, technicians also work with the electron and the elements of the tiniest known basic building blocks of nature, all of which are made up of atoms and their electrons. What a fantastic technology to be a part of and to understand.

Last, the opportunity for advancement is excellent for electronics technicians. Innovations in electronics, computers, and communications open many doors for those who might like to explore challenging work as senior technicians or engineers. Upward mobility or sliding into different types of work in electronics is common for technicians.

Get a job and get a rewarding career? Both are waiting for you in the field of electronics.

Dick Glass, CETsr, EHF
President, Electronics Technicians Association, International
Greencastle, Indiana
www.eta-i.org

# Acknowledgments

The author greatly appreciates the cooperation of the following in the researching and writing of this book:

American Electronics Association
Confederation College
Edison Community College
Electronics Technicians Association
Haywood Community College
Howard Community College
Institute of Electrical and Electronics Engineers
International Society of Certified Electronics Technicians
New River Community College
U.S. Department of Labor

# INTRODUCTION

OKAY, SO NOBODY claims that choosing a career is easy. After all, occupational choices are among the most important decisions anyone makes. These decisions should be made carefully and thoughtfully. You need to consider a variety of factors, because the decisions you make today can shape your life for years to come.

So, have you ever considered a career in electronics? This is one occupational area in which technological change provides great potential for men and women with the appropriate interests and aptitudes. Unlike many job areas that become displaced by advancing technology, electronics remains at the forefront of such change. This means that if you choose an electronics career and obtain the right training, chances are excellent that this background (combined with continuing education in the years ahead) will serve you well throughout your career.

For any reader interested in electronics, this book is offered as an overview of the basic facts needed in considering and planning for a career in this field. The material offered here should provide any interested person with a basic understanding of this challenging occupational area.

# 1

# THE IMPORTANCE
## OF ELECTRONICS

No MATTER WHERE you look, you'll find electronic devices. Consider just how wide-ranging the impact of electronics technology is on everyone's life today. For example, in the last week have you:

- Used a cell phone?
- Downloaded music?
- Watched television?
- Operated a computer?
- Used a portable or desktop calculator?
- Driven or ridden in an automobile?
- Used a microwave oven?
- Watched a DVD?
- Used an automatic teller machine?
- Listened to a radio or MP3 player?
- Checked the time with a digital watch or clock?

All of these functions, and many others too numerous to name, would be impossible without electronic components. Thanks to the many marvelous capabilities provided by electronics technology, hundreds of conveniences are made possible in the home, school, workplace, and elsewhere.

Think about how you spend the first few hours of an ordinary day. You get up at a preset time, thanks to a clock-radio that offers a variety of electronic functions. You may prepare breakfast with a microwave oven, watch the morning news on television, or check out the latest happenings online. Then you may ride to school or work in an automobile or bus that depends on computerized controls to start the engine and keep it running. During the morning, you may use a computer yourself or interact with someone else who does. If you visit a store or restaurant, the checkout process will depend on an electronic cash register. Ditto for any banking activities. Any information you receive—whether from radio, television, the Internet, newspapers, or textbooks—will have been transmitted, printed, or processed with electronic equipment. At any time, day or night, your life is enhanced by the practical applications of electronics.

Electronic devices don't just provide convenience. They also promote health, safety, and other serious matters. For example, hospitals use a variety of electronic devices in helping patients by diagnosing and treating illnesses. The military services, as has been so vividly demonstrated in televised reports of modern warfare, have been revolutionized by "smart" bombs, cruise missiles that can travel hundreds of miles with pinpoint precision, and other weapons based on advanced electronics.

Thanks to the growing role that electronic devices play in virtually all aspects of modern society, careers in electronics represent one of the most promising of all areas of employment. The ability to work with electronics is a valuable skill. Persons who can design, build, install, or repair electronic devices or components hold a wide range of interesting jobs.

A career in electronics can entail anything from working on an assembly line or making simple electronic components to helping design a complex piece of high-tech equipment. In many instances the work performed will be the repair of existing items rather than the development of new ones.

Whatever the tasks involved, working with electronics requires special knowledge and skills. As a result, women and men who have acquired these capabilities often find themselves in an advantageous position when it comes to seeking good jobs and pursuing challenging careers.

## Electronics Versus Electricity

Before reviewing the subject of electronics further, it is important to make a distinction between careers in electricity and those in electronics. These two terms are sometimes used interchangeably, but there are usually some basic differences.

Both deal with electric current, and, of course, there could be no electronic devices without the power provided by electricity. But from a technical and career viewpoint, the two fields deal with the use of electric current in different ways.

Electricians and related workers generally handle equipment that is based on the flow of current, while persons working in electronics concentrate on devices based on short pulses of electricity. An electronic device changes the current's direction or frequency to make it function as a signal that represents sounds, images, numbers, or other information. This basic difference separates many kinds of electrical and electronic items.

Electricians, for example, tend to work with electric motors, transformers, electric lighting, and so forth. A typical job performed by an electrician might be installing the wiring in a new house or office building or rewiring a large motor used in an industrial setting.

Technicians and others involved in electronics tend to deal with devices such as microprocessors and other equipment using integrated circuits. For example, a career in electronics may involve working with computers, digital entertainment devices, or broadcasting equipment.

A basic understanding of electricity is needed by anyone who works in electronics, and the distinction between the two concepts is not uniformly observed. But in choosing educational programs, applying for jobs, or other activities, it is important to be aware of the general boundaries of each field.

## Development of Electronics

The development of electronics is a recent part of human history. Although the existence of electricity has been recognized (if not fully understood) for hundreds of years, the rise of electronics has occurred only in about the last century.

The invention of gas-discharge tubes in the late 1800s and the later development of vacuum tubes contributed to the growth of electronics. The first widespread application of tubes began in the 1920s in radio, which helped usher in the modern world. Vacuum tubes were also instrumental in the development of television and early computers.

In the late 1940s and early 1950s, the development of solid-state technology greatly accelerated the growth of electronics. Solid-state devices, in which a signal passes through a solid material instead of through a vacuum, represented a great improvement over technology based on vacuum tubes. Even more revolutionary was the invention in the early 1960s of integrated circuits, in which tiny chips of silicon or some other semiconductor material could do the same work as a bulky transistor. This technology led to the development of microprocessors and the advanced electronic devices we enjoy today.

Certainly over the last few decades, the growth of electronics technology has expanded tremendously, and more and more sophisticated electronic items have begun to play an important part in everyday life.

Some of the most important influences on the development of electronics technologies have included the following.

- The development of radio, television, facsimile (fax) machines, and other means of communicating over distances
- Advances in transportation, including air and space travel
- The invention and growing use of computers in virtually all aspects of life, including the rapid expansion of the Internet
- Developments in warfare and military technology, with various sophisticated weapons and weapons systems demanding new and improved uses of electronics
- The growing uses of electronic devices in home entertainment
- The invention of robots and automated manufacturing processes
- Changes in design and production of electronic devices, which have made them more affordable and thus more widely available

## Advantages of a Career in Electronics

A career in electronics offers a number of potential benefits. These advantages include the following.

### Good Salaries and Wages

Most people who work in the field of electronics earn salaries or wages that compare quite favorably with other fields. In fact, some jobs in this area bring salaries that are significantly higher than the average for all occupations. Because many of these jobs require special knowledge and skills, employers often will pay excellent salaries or wages to attract employees who possess the necessary background. In some cases, electronics personnel can earn several times the average compensation paid to unskilled workers.

Also, men and women employed in electronics may receive a variety of attractive fringe benefits. Such benefits may include medical insurance, retirement plans, vacation pay, support to pursue additional education, profit sharing, or other benefits. Earnings and benefits are discussed in Chapter 8.

### Long-Range Job Potential

It may sound trite to claim that electronics represents the wave of the future, but there is a great deal of truth in such a statement. After all, it would be difficult to pick an area where more potential for the future exists. Recent changes in electronics have been so immense that people often compare today's reality to the vision of some science fiction writers of decades past, and experts predict even more fantastic changes in the future. People in all walks of life depend heavily on the work performed by specialists in electronics, and this trend is expected not only to continue, but to grow.

In choosing a career, an important factor should be its potential to survive in a rapidly changing world. Unfortunately for the persons holding them, many jobs disappear forever as they are displaced by changing technology and economic conditions.

Although this is a possibility in any field, it seems less likely in electronics than in many other career areas. This is a field that tends to thrive on change. Many jobs in electronics are close to what some experts call the cutting edge of advancing technology. As a result, electronics is less vulnerable to change than many other career areas.

### Challenging Work Assignments

Would you rather design microchips in an electronics lab or shelve bags of potato chips in a grocery store? Of course, there is a great deal of room between one extreme and the other, and there is nothing wrong with working in a store or performing other respectable work that may require little or no special knowledge or training. However, many workers in unskilled jobs find their work boring and without a sense of challenge, as well as less rewarding in terms of income, benefits, and future potential.

Persons employed in electronics, on the other hand, often find the work itself truly interesting. Designing an electronic device or diagnosing and repairing an equipment problem can provide variety, mental stimulation, and a high degree of job satisfaction.

### Comfortable Work Environment

Most work performed by people employed in electronics takes place indoors. This might consist of any of a number of settings including a workroom in a small business, a shop or laboratory in an engineering firm, or various locations within a large manufacturing plant. In some cases, the workplace will be the same each day; in others, job assignments will involve moving from one location to another. For example, a technician might travel to different businesses or visit people's homes to service or repair electronic equipment. Such an arrangement can be particularly interesting for men and women who enjoy change and variety in their daily routine.

In any instance, working in electronics usually offers the advantage of comfortable environments and relatively low levels of physical exertion, compared to highly physical jobs such as construction work, farming, or heavy industrial production.

## *Mobility*

Once you obtain skills in electronics, they can serve you virtually anywhere in the civilized world as well as in your home community. This means that you need not move far away to find a good job, unless you live in a remote rural area where technical job opportunities are limited. If you prefer to explore new locations, the chances are excellent of landing a job that will take you to a new city, state, or province of your choice.

After all, most electronic fields represent areas where skilled workers are in high demand. So if you acquire the necessary training and skills, you should be able to find a job nearly anywhere.

## *Wide Range of Educational Choices*

Although some type of training probably will be needed, you can choose from a variety of educational options. A bachelor's degree may be needed to pursue a career in electronic engineering, but many technicians' jobs require far less training. In fact, many educational programs take two years or fewer to complete.

In addition, you can choose formal training in a school or college or another approach such as an apprenticeship or on-the-job training program. The end result is that you can select the type of educational program that best suits your own abilities and preferences. (Educational choices are detailed in Chapter 7.)

## Reviewing Options

The options for a career in electronics are many. To learn more, consult the following chapters.

Chapter 2 provides an overview of the types of careers available, along with a look at future prospects. Chapter 3 covers repair of home entertainment equipment, and repair of industrial electronics equipment is discussed in Chapter 4.

Chapter 5 looks at electronics engineering and engineering technology, and several specialized career areas are discussed in Chapter 6. Training programs are discussed in Chapter 7, while earnings and benefits are covered in Chapter 8.

Chapter 9 examines special certifications and electronics organizations, and Chapter 10 concludes with observations on the wide range of opportunities offered by a career in electronics plus advice on landing a job in the field.

Several appendixes are also provided, including information on schools and colleges providing appropriate training programs.

## 2

# ELECTRONICS IN THE TWENTY-FIRST CENTURY

IF YOU WORK in electronics, you'll be connected to some of the most rapidly changing areas of modern technology. The entire computer arena, for example, is linked to the advances of electronics. The same is true of various industries ranging from communications to transportation. With the vital role that electronics plays in so many areas, the future of the field holds great promise.

## Career Possibilities

Men and women who work in electronics hold a wide range of jobs. These include the following major categories of employment:

- Repairing electronic equipment used primarily in home entertainment

- Repairing and maintaining electronic equipment for commercial and industrial use
- Designing, testing, and supervising the manufacture of electronic equipment
- Operating, servicing, or repairing equipment in specialized areas such as broadcasting

A brief description of each area follows, and more details about these occupations are provided in later chapters. Resources for further reading on electronics careers are given in the end of the book.

## Repair and Installation of Home Entertainment Equipment

With the proliferation of electronic devices and systems used for personal entertainment or home convenience, an entire support industry of installing, servicing, and repairing such equipment has arisen and expanded.

Among the first workers of this type were radio repair persons, and after that, those who provided the same type of services for television sets. Today, technicians known as electronic home equipment repairers (or simply as service technicians or electronic technicians, or sometimes as home technology integrators) work with a variety of electronic devices found in the home—for example, home entertainment systems, microwave ovens, and home security systems.

These technicians install new equipment, service working equipment, and repair malfunctioning items. Some specialize in a single type of equipment, such as DVD players, while others work with a variety of equipment types. Their jobs involve not just the technical tasks involved, but also the human relations element of dealing directly with customers and, in some cases, going into private residences to provide on-site installation or service.

Technicians in this area may be self-employed operators of their own small businesses, or they may work for various types of employers, including small or medium-sized companies specializing in equipment and repair services or large retail firms that sell electronic equipment and then provide the support services needed to keep it in good working order.

## Repair of Commercial and Industrial Electronic Equipment

Technicians who install and repair electronic equipment for businesses and other organizations fall under the general category of commercial and industrial electronics technicians. They may also be identified as industrial electronics technicians or other similar titles.

Men and women employed in this area work with equipment such as antennas, automated manufacturing equipment controls, radar systems, guidance controls for rockets and missiles, industrial robots, and diagnostic equipment used in hospitals and other medical facilities.

They are employed throughout the United States and Canada in a variety of industries. This includes working for large corporations, smaller companies, and other organizations ranging from health care agencies and educational institutions to government agencies and the military.

## Electronics Engineering and Engineering Technology

At the opposite end of the spectrum from equipment repair is the design and manufacture of electronic systems, devices, and components. These functions are performed by engineers and engineering technologists or technicians.

Engineers, who require the highest level of education of the careers discussed here (usually at least a bachelor's degree), develop, test, and oversee the production or installation of electronic devices or systems. They may specialize in different areas such as radar systems, computer design, electronic controls used in automated manufacturing, or development of sound equipment.

Engineering technologists and technicians perform similar work but usually under the supervision of engineers. While engineers may be heavily involved in the theory behind a given engineering problem, the technologist or technician generally plays a more hands-on role. For example, a person in this area may assemble a piece of equipment that has been designed by an engineer, and then the two may work together to test and improve it.

Positions in both areas can be found in the United States and Canada in a range of industries as well as in the military services.

## Specialized Electronics Areas

A number of careers provide opportunities to specialize in one type of electronic equipment or within a single industry.

### Broadcasting

Broadcast technicians work in radio and television, operating and maintaining recording and transmitting equipment.

### Computer Service and Repair

Another specialty area is computer service and repair. With computers playing an increasingly central role throughout most segments of society, a growing demand exists for persons who can maintain and repair them.

Computer service technicians provide this function for companies that sell computer equipment as well as for organizations large enough to hire their own staff for this purpose. These technicians service and repair not only the computers themselves, but also such related equipment as various types of printers. They also install computer systems and test them for defects.

### Other Areas

Workers in several other areas also provide specialized services that include applications in electronics. Positions as communications equipment mechanics, elevator installers and repairers, home appliance and power tool repairers, office machine and cash register servicers, telephone installers, and vending machine servicers and repairers are but a few.

## Job Titles

Among the job titles identified by the U.S. Department of Labor in electronics are:

Bench technician
Computer repairer
Computer service technician
Electromechanical assembler
Electromechanical technician

Electromedical-equipment repairer
Electronic-communications technician
Electronic-component processor
Electronic production-line maintenance mechanic
Electronic sales-and-service technician
Electronics assembler
Electronics assembler, prototype
Electronics-design engineer
Electronics inspector
Electronics mechanic
Electronics-research engineer
Electronics technician
Electronics technician, nuclear reactor
Electronics test engineer
Electronics tester
Electronics utility worker
Field technician

## Background and Skills Needed

Electronics careers may hold significant promise, but it is important to keep individual abilities and interests in mind when considering the various options available. Just as in other occupations, not everyone is well suited to an electronics career.

In considering the possibilities, take into account the following factors. Most people should possess (or be able to develop) most or all of the following traits to work effectively in electronics and to enjoy the experience.

1. **The ability to work with hand tools.** This might vary from screwdrivers or soldering guns to voltage meters, but the ability to

use tools and items such as meters and scopes—or to learn to use them well—is definitely a must for all but the most theoretical work in electronics.

2. **Good math skills.** This is more important in engineering than in many service jobs, but any study of the theory behind electronics requires that information be expressed and understood in mathematical terms. Persons who enjoy math and are good at it have a real edge in this field. For those who feel they lack math abilities, it may be possible to improve the situation through remedial courses or other efforts.

3. **An aptitude for solving problems.** Much work in electronics revolves around the solving of problems. A new design for an electronic component that does not work as planned or a malfunctioning control system in a manufacturing plant's assembly line, for example, presents problems that must be solved. If you like to work Sodoku or crossword puzzles, figure out ways of fixing cars or household appliances, or even outwit computer games, these may be signs of such an aptitude. Special tests available from counselors also can help determine aptitudes in this direction.

4. **A willingness to learn.** Electronics is a complicated subject. To succeed in this area, you must be willing to learn fundamentals as well as a variety of practical applications. This usually means reading and studying textbooks and manuals as well as putting in practice time in a shop or laboratory setting. Such efforts may take place within any number of settings, ranging from vocational schools or colleges to on-the-job training programs. Whatever the type of instruction involved, the time and energy needed to master it must be something you are willing to commit.

5. **Patience and attention to detail.** The work involved in electronics seldom can be hurried. Instead, it requires patient adherence to details that might seem trivial to the uninformed observer.

But considering the delicate and precise nature of much electronic equipment and the safety factors involved in devices that utilize electricity, patience and attention to detail are absolutely necessary.

Certainly, your basic abilities and aptitudes are only part of the equation for a successful career in electronics. Many other factors also are involved, and these details are reviewed in subsequent chapters. But if, after assessing your own potential, you feel optimistic about an electronics career, the opportunity to follow up on this ambition awaits you.

## Future Prospects

A career in electronics can offer a bright future. Studies conducted by the U.S. Department of Labor have found that in some career areas related to electronics, growth in new jobs is expected to occur by up to 26 percent in the decade ending in 2014. In other areas, less rapid growth is expected. Actual prospects will vary according to a number of factors including the specialty within the electronics fields, technology trends, growth or stagnation in the national or local economy, and other factors. For example, overall employment of electrical and electronics installers and repairers is expected to grow by up to 8 percent during the period ending in 2014, according to the U.S. Department of Labor. This is a slower rate than the average for all occupations, but it is still significant. The same is true of electronic home entertainment equipment installers and repairers (for more details regarding projected job growth in specific areas, see later chapters).

In general, job opportunities related to electronics should be best for applicants who have a thorough knowledge of electrical equipment and electronics as well as a specialty such as equipment repair, installation practices, engineering technology, or some other area. Even in areas where job growth is limited, the need to replace workers who transfer to other occupations or leave the labor force will result in numerous job openings.

Not only will jobs be available for those who are qualified, but this field represents one of the most promising areas for the future in terms of new and interesting developments. Enormous changes have occurred in recent years in the way electronic devices affect everyone's life. Even more can be expected in the future. For those who pursue careers in electronics, the potential exists to be at the cutting edge of technological development.

# 3

# Installation and Repair of Electronic Home Entertainment Equipment

What home in North America has no electronic equipment? In most families, a normal part of everyday life is entertainment provided through electronic means. The result is that persons who enjoy hands-on work with electronics can pursue a challenging career in servicing and repairing equipment used in the home. This career area has broadened in recent years in response to the growing popularity of various types of home entertainment based on electronic equipment.

An American or Canadian family may own any number of electronic devices used primarily for entertainment purposes. The great majority of homes have at least one television set, for example, and many have two or more, including big-screen models. DVD players and recorders have become commonplace. In homes with children, electronic games are hardly more unusual than baseballs or dolls. Radios, MP3 players, compact disc players, and other types of musical equipment enrich the lives of people of all ages.

With these and other items becoming an increasingly integral part of everyday home life, the need to install, service, and repair electronic equipment of this type is an expanding one. After all, even the best equipment is not indestructible. Parts become dirty or wear out, units become damaged though household accidents or improper care, and routine maintenance must be performed. Yet because of the complex nature of most electronic components, only a specially trained technician can perform the required work. When this need is combined with the large volume of electronic equipment used for home entertainment, the result is a career area with significant potential.

## Work Performed

Men and women who work as electronic home equipment repairers also may be known as service technicians or electronics technicians, or in some cases as home technology integrators. They install equipment, link items through computer technology, service equipment that is still functioning properly, diagnose problems, and make repairs.

The kinds of equipment they install or repair varies. They work with devices such as televisions, radios, stereo components, video and audio disc players, video cameras, and video recorders. Technicians specializing in equipment used in the home also work with home security systems, intercom equipment, satellite television dishes, and home theater systems. The latter typically include components such as large-screen televisions and sophisticated surround-sound audio components.

Work performed on other electronic items not actually used for entertainment also may fit into this area. For example, service technicians may work with microwave ovens or other kitchen appliances, burglar alarms, and multifaceted home security systems.

In carrying out their work, these technicians may perform tasks such as:

- Reading service manuals or wiring diagrams
- Running a multipart check of the various components of an electronic device or system
- Installing and integrating electronic equipment
- Identifying defective parts
- Replacing worn or broken parts
- Operating testing equipment such as oscilloscopes or voltage meters
- Making adjustments in electronic controls
- Cutting or connecting wires
- Joining metal components together with a soldering gun
- Removing or installing solid-state electronic components
- Operating a variety of tools and equipment ranging from pliers and screwdrivers to signal generators and frequency counters
- Lifting or transporting equipment
- Driving a car, truck, or van to make service calls
- Talking with customers to determine problems or explain repairs
- Writing reports about servicing or repairs
- Calculating bills for parts and service

Men and women who work in this field must be able to concentrate on the task at hand and to work methodically and carefully. They must evaluate problems with equipment and then determine the appropriate course of action. In many instances, they also need to communicate effectively with customers.

In many ways, the work performed by service technicians is similar to that of technicians employed in industry. Persons who have been trained for work in industry, or who have been employed in the commercial sector, may find it relatively easy to branch off into this career area if they so choose. The same is true of those who have been trained in electronics in the military.

## Places of Employment

Men and women who make their living repairing home electronic equipment are employed throughout North America. Many jobs can be found in metropolitan areas, where the population is large. Others can be found in smaller cities and towns where retail stores selling electronic equipment are located or where there is sufficient population to support a service or repair business.

Employers in this field include:

- Large department stores that maintain their own service departments
- Stores specializing in musical equipment, home appliances, or a range of electronic equipment
- Businesses that do not sell equipment but specialize in some combination of installation, repair, and service
- Self-operated businesses

The latter represents a promising alternative for those persons who prefer to operate their own businesses rather than work for another employer. Some service technicians work out of their homes, where they maintain a shop located in a basement, garage, or workroom dedicated to this purpose. Others operate out of a shop or store they build, buy, or lease. They may serve as the only technician or may hire others who work under their supervision. In this case, their duties may include supervising employees, completing business reports, and other managerial functions.

## Working Environment

Service technicians and related workers usually perform their jobs in comfortable working environments. This might consist of a shop setting to which customers bring their equipment for repairs and service, or in some cases, it might mean going into people's homes to provide on-site work. In either case, technicians in this field avoid the discomfort faced by some workers of having a job outdoors or in a noisy, assembly-line setting.

A typical shop setting will include good lighting, heating or air-conditioning, and workbenches or counters designed for easy access. In some cases, the environment is quite informal, and technicians may be allowed to listen to radios or media players while working. Informal, comfortable clothes are also the norm, although some companies may ask workers to wear smocks or some type of standardized clothing. For self-employed technicians, all of these factors are determined according to the worker's own preferences.

For technicians who go to customers' homes to make service calls, working environments will vary. Some people enjoy this kind of variety in work settings. One job might take them to an apartment building, another to a huge mansion, and another to a house in the suburbs. At the same time, they come in contact with many different people of all ages and backgrounds. For people who easily become bored working in the same setting, this can be a real plus. Even the time spent driving to and from job sites can provide a change of pace. Of course, for those who prefer a highly structured setting, these same factors can become liabilities rather than assets.

Technicians sometimes may need to move or carry heavy items, such as television sets or microwave ovens, so they must guard against injuries caused from lifting or dropping equipment or from falling while moving larger items. They also need to observe careful safety procedures to avoid electrical shock or burns. In general, however, this is not a particularly hazardous career area.

## The Right Skills and Aptitudes

Persons who hope to work in home entertainment equipment repair should have the same basic aptitudes as those who plan to work in industry. These include:

- Problem-solving abilities
- The ability to work with hand tools, electronic measurement devices, and other tools and equipment
- Sufficient math skills to complete required courses and understand basic electronic theory
- Patience
- Good working habits

In addition, it helps to have good human relations skills. Quite often, technicians must discuss equipment problems with owners, explain the nature of repairs, estimate costs, and interact in other ways. Those who get along well with other people and communicate effectively may have a special advantage in working in this field.

## Getting Trained

To prepare for a career in this field, some type of training will be necessary. Such instruction might come in the form of on-the-job training or an apprenticeship. For example, the service division of a large retail firm may hire a person who has had little or no special training in electronics and then provide short-term classes or assign the individual to assist experienced workers and learn repair techniques in the process. This can be a relatively informal training program or a more formal apprenticeship, although the latter is not as common in this specialty area as in the commercial and industrial area.

Many persons prepare for this field by attending a vocational school, trade school, or two-year college. Some programs, especially those in noncollegiate vocational schools, concentrate on a single area such as television repair. Others provide several options from which students can select.

For example, students who attend Ohio's Edison Community College can acquire these skills in several different ways.

1. By taking electronics courses of their choice to gain specialized knowledge but without pursuing a formal program of study.

2. By pursuing a certificate program that consists almost entirely of electronics and related courses and can be completed in a year of full-time study.

3. By completing an associate degree (two-year) program that includes not only electronics courses, but also other subjects designed to enhance their background. Students can select from a program designed primarily for transfer to a four-year school or an electronics technology degree. With the latter, options in control systems and in industrial systems are available.

Many courses in the associate degree programs are transferable to four-year colleges and universities, although their primary purpose is job preparation rather than transferability. Students completing these programs have gone on to attend Bowling Green State University, the University of Dayton, the University of Toledo, and a number of others. Although persons planning to work as service technicians may not pursue additional education, the fact that courses may be transferred is valuable if future plans change.

At Edison, as at many other two-year colleges, the programs are designed to meet a wide range of employment objectives in the electrical/electronics field. Many such programs are categorized in areas such as electronics, electrical/electronics technology, or electronics technology, rather than by a specific job area. This means that you may not find a program offered specifically for those who plan to work as service technicians, but you instead will take the knowledge learned in a broad-based electronics program and apply it to your field. It also means you will be studying with people who plan to work in industry and in various specialized areas of electronics and, in some cases, with workers who are already employed but updating or expanding their skills. The result can be a positive environment to share information and learn as much as possible about the subjects being covered, especially in a lab setting where you may work in tandem with other students.

For those who want to earn an industrial electronics technology degree, two typical sequences of study may be followed. One option is control systems.

### First Semester
DC Circuits
AC Circuits
Industrial Controls
Industrial Safety and Troubleshooting
Mechanical Systems
College Algebra

### Second Semester
Introduction to Spreadsheets
Electronic Devices
Digital Electronics
Programmable Logic Controllers
English Composition I
Trigonometry

### Third Semester
Electronic Circuits
Servo Systems and Robotics
Electronics Project I
Advanced Programmable Logic Controllers
Hydraulics and Pneumatics
Technical Writing

*Fourth Semester*
Electrical Power and Control
Controls Project I
Effective Communication
Humanities elective
Social/behavioral science elective

The other option is industrial systems.

*First Semester*
DC Circuits
AC Circuits
Industrial Controls
Industrial Safety and Troubleshooting
Mechanical Systems
English Composition I
Trigonometry

*Second Semester*
Electronic Devices
Digital Electronics
Programmable Logic Controllers
Print Reading and Sketching
Personal Computer Applications

*Third Semester*
Servo Systems and Robotics
Electronics Project I
Hydraulics and Pneumatics
Technical Writing

Technical specialization elective
Humanities elective

***Fourth Semester***
Machine Reliability
Applied Industrial Troubleshooting
Effective Communication
Survey of Manufacturing Processes
Social/behavioral science elective

For most jobs in repairing home equipment, the background gained through a one-year certificate program will provide all the basic skills necessary to find a job and to perform well on the job. The extra courses covered under an associate degree program, although not usually required for service technicians, could nevertheless prove helpful from both an educational standpoint and for potential use in the future. In either case, a completed degree or certificate should give you a competitive edge over persons who have not had such training.

Several of these electronics courses would have special appeal to those who are interested in careers as service technicians. For example, in the Electronic Devices course, students learn about semiconductor diodes, transistors, and field effect transistors (FETs). The course also covers bias stability requirements and analysis of bias circuitry; operational characteristics of FET and diode switching circuits; and component testing and evaluation.

In Digital Electronics, students learn the fundamentals of digital electronics. The course includes number systems and codes peculiar to digital systems, design and analysis of combinational logic circuitry, and other basics.

Other courses cover various aspects of electronics, many of which can be applied to the home equipment repair field.

Programs and courses of this type vary from one school to another, but they are widely available. More details on selecting a school or college are provided in Chapter 7.

## Employment Outlook

According to the U.S. Department of Labor, future job growth for electronic home entertainment equipment installers and repairers may be limited by technological developments that have lowered the price and improved the reliability of equipment; thus when malfunctions do occur, it often is cheaper for consumers to replace equipment than to pay for repairs. Nevertheless, growth of up to 8 percent is expected for the decade ending in 2014. While some job openings will come about because of employment growth, many other openings will result from the need to replace workers who retire or who take other jobs. Opportunities will be best for applicants with formal training in electronics and with related hands-on experience.

Projections are that employment growth will be spurred somewhat by the increased use of sophisticated digital equipment such as DVDs, high-definition digital televisions, and digital camcorders. There also will be demand to install sophisticated home entertainment systems.

# 4

# COMMERCIAL AND INDUSTRIAL ELECTRONICS EQUIPMENT REPAIR

FOR AN AREA of high demand for electronics technicians, try the installation and repair of equipment for businesses, the military, or other organizations. People who perform this function may be designated as commercial and industrial electronics technicians or, more simply, as industrial electronics technicians.

## Job Tasks

Working in this area may involve completing tasks such as:

- Installing electronic components of a radar system at a commercial airport
- Setting up special electronic equipment used to diagnose illnesses in hospitals

- Repairing components of an automated assembly line in a manufacturing plant
- Cleaning and servicing an industrial robot
- Repairing a malfunctioning component of a missile tracking system at a military base
- Installing a radio transmitter for a new radio station

In industrial settings, electronic sensors monitor the equipment used in manufacturing and other processes, providing feedback to the programmable logic control (PLC), which controls the equipment. Among other duties, technicians work with PLCs to make sure they efficiently process the information provided by the sensors and make adjustments to optimize output. Many installers and repairers, known as field technicians, travel to factories or other locations to repair PLCs and other electronic equipment. Bench technicians, on the other hand, work in repair shops located in factories and service centers, repairing components that cannot be fixed at the factory or industrial site.

In many cases, installers replace old electronic control units with new PLCs. This may involve installing different sensors and electrically powered devices and writing computer programs for the installation.

Some installers and repairers specialize in working with communications or transportation equipment such as sound, sonar, security, navigation, and surveillance systems on trains, watercraft, or other vehicles. Others focus on installation and repair of communication, sound, security, and navigation equipment in motor vehicles. Much of this work involves new alarm or sound systems, such as replacing a radio unit with a new CD or MP3 player. Other tasks include installing or repairing global positioning systems used in motor vehicle navigation.

Completion of these and other related tasks may require the ability to:

- Use electronic tools such as ohmmeters, voltage meters, oscilloscopes, and signal generators
- Use simple hand tools such as pliers, wire cutters, or screwdrivers
- Read blueprints, wiring diagrams, or equipment specifications
- Maintain logs of service and repairs for a specific system or piece of equipment
- Test and calibrate electronic components
- Identify reasons equipment has malfunctioned
- Replace defective electronic components
- Install or replace wiring for an electronic system
- Clean dirty parts of a piece of equipment or an entire system

Technicians working in this field may perform a wide range of jobs. They might repair computers, industrial controls, radar systems, telemetering and missile control systems, transmitters, antennas, servomechanisms, or other electronic devices or systems. In the process, they might operate diagnostic equipment to test faulty devices or components and diagnose the causes of malfunctions. Related tasks described by the U.S. Department of Labor include the following.

> Tests electronic components and circuits to locate defects, using oscilloscopes, signal generators, ammeters, and voltmeters. Replaces

defective components and wiring and adjusts mechanical parts, using hand tools and soldering iron. Aligns, adjusts, and calibrates equipment according to specifications. Calibrates testing instruments. Maintains records of repairs, calibrations, and tests. May install equipment in industrial or military establishments and in aircraft and missiles. May operate equipment, such as communication equipment and missile control systems, in ground and flight tests, and be required to hold a license from a governmental agency.

## Working Conditions

Electronics technicians work in a variety of settings. A typical job site might be a room or shop area devoted to repair and servicing of equipment. Such an environment usually will feature good lighting, controlled levels of temperature and humidity, and an overall work setting that is consistently comfortable. The work environment is generally somewhat casual, where employees wear informal clothes and feel free to talk among themselves or play soft music while working.

Not all jobs or tasks are performed in such a setting, however. Technicians may repair or service equipment where it is used rather than in a central servicing facility. This situation can take workers to a wide range of settings, such as assembly lines, different offices within a large organization, manufacturing facilities, construction sites, military bases, or other locations where electronic equipment is used. Inevitably, some sites will be less pleasant than others, but an offsetting factor is the variety workers may enjoy in the process.

In general, electronics technicians can count on favorable working conditions. Because electronic devices may be sensitive to humidity, temperature extremes, and other environmental features, they usually are located in areas that also are comfortable to human beings. The end result is that technicians usually avoid the discomfort sometimes experienced by those who must work outdoors or in other physically challenging settings.

## Educational Background

Persons who hope to work as electronic technicians in the industrial or commercial sector should demonstrate most or all of the aptitudes discussed previously. Of particular importance is an orientation to addressing and solving problems.

In addition, some type of training generally will be necessary to work in this field. This might consist of vocational classes offered at the high school level or through an adult education program, training in a technical or proprietary school, an apprenticeship, or on-the-job training.

A frequent path to a career in this area is completion of an electronics program offered by a two-year college. Such programs are offered in many community, junior, and technical colleges.

For example, Delaware County Community College located in Media, Pennsylvania, offers an associate degree program in electronics technology. The program, which can be completed in two years of full-time study, prepares students to perform such tasks as the following:

- Identify malfunctions in electrical and electromechanical instruments
- Repair nonfunctioning electrical and electromechanical instruments
- Calibrate scientific and industrial instruments

- Use established maintenance procedures for scientific and industrial instruments
- Test input/output parameters of electrical/mechanical devices
- Assemble electrical and electromechanical devices
- Identify electrical/electromechanical components, devices, or systems in accordance with predetermined specifications
- Present technical information in oral, written, and graphic form, including use of microcomputers to manipulate content and access information

A typical course of study under this program would extend over four academic semesters as follows, although students can take longer than two years if they desire to attend part-time or simply take fewer courses at any one time.

*First Semester*
English Composition I
Technical Mathematics I
Technical Communications
DC Analysis
Humanities elective

*Second Semester*
Technical Mathematics II
Technical Physics I
Electronics I
Digital Electronics
English Composition II

*Third Semester*
AC Analysis
Electronics II
Electromechanical Systems
Electronics Troubleshooting and Repair
101 Technical Physics II

*Fourth Semester*
Microprocessors I
Technical elective
Social sciences elective
Introduction to Interpersonal Communication
Career elective

The content of electronics courses such as these provides students with detailed background in the key areas needed to work in industry following program completion. For example, those students enrolling in Electronics I learn to perform tasks such as the following:

- Analyze the behavior of simple diode circuits
- Analyze the behavior of single-stage transistor amplifier circuits and of single-stage field-effect amplifier circuits
- Follow schematic diagrams to connect simple circuits
- Build DC rectifier circuits and measure their ripple factor
- Build single-stage transistor amplifier circuits and measure their gain
- Test diodes, transistors, and field-effect transistors for proper operation

In the Digital Electronics course, students learn about digital techniques and circuits, including the operation of digital logic gates as well as integrated circuit families used in digital equipment. By the end of the course, successful students are able to:

- Discuss the applications and advantages in using digital techniques
- Implement logic functions using standard digital logic gates
- Discuss the operation of flip-flops, counters, and shift registers
- Design elementary digital circuits

At Haywood Community College in Clyde, North Carolina, students in electronic engineering technology generally take the following courses in addition to general studies courses in areas such as expository writing, speech, and social or behavioral sciences.

*First Year*
Technical Drafting I
Introduction to Computers
Introduction to Technology
C++ Programming
DC/AC Circuit Analysis
Algebra/Trigonometry I or Precalculus Algebra

*Summer Semester*
Algebra/Trigonometry II or Precalculus Trigonometry
Electronic Devices
Industrial Controls

**Second Year**
Introduction to PLC
CAD for Electronics
Digital Electronics
Physics-Mechanics
Linear IC Applications
Introduction to Microprocessors
Lasers and Applications
Technical electives

Not all two-year colleges offer programs in electronics, but most technical colleges and many community colleges include such programs among their standard offerings. Many also feature their own variations of electronics programs in areas such as industrial electronics or in communication technology. Other colleges may offer options in automation instrumentation, fiber optics communications, or other areas. To determine what is available at any college, consult its website or catalog, or contact the admissions office or the electronics department.

## Skills and Traits Needed

If you think a career in this area sounds appealing, consider if you have (or can develop) the following skills or traits.

- Ability and enjoyment in working with your hands
- Ability to work with tools
- Curiosity about technical matters (for example, wondering how a certain device works)

- Ability to handle the math involved in understanding electronics
- Satisfaction with working in an industrial or commercial environment, spending most of your time working on electronic equipment
- Patience
- Good eyesight (or the kind of vision limitations that can be corrected with glasses or contact lenses)
- Ability to understand technical material such as blueprints, diagrams, and manuals
- At least a high school education
- A willingness to complete additional education

If you possess most or all of these traits (or are confident you can develop them), then a career in commercial or industrial equipment repair may be well worth pursuing.

## Employment Outlook

According to the U.S. Department of Labor, job growth for those specializing in repairing commercial and industrial electronics equipment may reach between 9 and 17 percent for the decade ending in 2014. Many job openings will come about because of employment growth. Other positions will become available as current workers retire or take other jobs. As in other related career areas, opportunities will be best for applicants who have completed specialized training in electronics and those with related hands-on experience.

# 5

# Electronics Engineering and Engineering Technology

Some of the most interesting careers in electronics can be found in the areas of engineering and engineering technology. Electronics engineers and technologists perform a wide range of important functions.

## Engineering Versus Engineering Technology

Although terminology can be confusing, some basic differences exist between these two areas, both of which also differ from other electronics occupations discussed in previous chapters.

Electronics engineering technologists (also sometimes called technicians, although their work may be on a different level than service technicians or related workers) perform work that in some ways is similar to that done by engineers but differs in that it usually involves applications more than theory. In other words, it has more of a hands-on focus. For instance, an engineer may design a new component or piece of equipment used on an automated assembly line. The new design is turned over to an engineering technologist, who installs the new component and tests its capabilities.

Generally, less education is required to become an engineering technologist, although this is not always the case. Many community and technical colleges offer associate degrees in electronics engineering technology or related areas, which can be completed in two years of full-time study. Most engineering degrees, on the other hand, take at least four years as a full-time student to complete. More information on these programs and other educational options is covered in Chapter 7.

Because more education is needed and responsibilities may be greater, the following statements often are true for electronics engineering when compared to engineering technology:

- Electronics engineering may be a more difficult field to enter, with many colleges requiring that students have excellent high school grades and high scores on standardized tests (such as the ACT or SAT exam) just to get admitted to an engineering program.
- Some engineering courses are more difficult than corresponding courses in engineering technology. A deeper understanding of math and physics may be necessary.
- Not only is the minimum educational level for electronics engineers a bachelor's degree, but many engineers also hold master's degrees or other advanced degrees.

- Engineers tend to earn the highest salaries of any electronics occupations.
- Engineers are more likely to move into management positions than those holding other types of electronics positions.

## Engineering Technologists

Persons functioning as engineering technologists or technicians often work under the supervision of engineers, or they may work in close coordination with other types of personnel.

Most typically, they lay out, build, test, troubleshoot, repair, or modify various types of electronic equipment such as computers, missile-control instrumentation, or machine tool numerical controls, to name just a few. In the process, they may discuss layout and assembly problems with electronics engineers and prepare sketches or computer-generated schematics to clarify design details and functional criteria of electronic units. They may also assemble experimental circuitry, complete prototype models, or recommend changes in circuitry or installation specifications to simplify assembly and maintenance. Technologists and technicians may also conduct a variety of tests to evaluate the performance and reliability of prototypes or production models.

Other duties that are described by the U.S. Department of Labor include:

Recommends changes in circuitry or installation specifications to simplify assembly and maintenance. Sets up standard test apparatus or contrives test equipment and circuitry; conducts functional, operational, environmental, and life tests to evaluate performance and reliability of prototype or production model. Analyzes and interprets test data. Adjusts, calibrates, aligns, and modifies circuitry and components and records effects on unit performance. Writes technical reports and develops charts, graphs, and schematics to describe and illustrate system operating characteristics, malfunctions, deviations from design specifications, and functional limitations for consideration by professional engineering personnel in broader determinations affecting system design and laboratory procedures. May operate bench lathes, drills, and other machine tools to fabricate nonprocurable items, such as coils, terminal boards, and chassis. May check out newly installed equipment in airplanes, ships, and structures to evaluate system performance under actual operating conditions. May instruct and supervise lower grade technical personnel. May be designated according to specialization in electronic applications.

Typical jobs undertaken by an electronics engineering technician may include:

- Assisting an engineer in designing a prototype for a new kind of medical testing equipment
- Writing specifications for a key component of a radar system
- Assembling a controlling device for an automated manufacturing system
- Diagnosing a problem in malfunctioning radio equipment
- Adjusting and improving movement of an industrial robot
- Writing a computer program as part of an automated manufacturing production line
- Repairing a piece of malfunctioning navigation equipment
- Using computer-aided design (CAD) techniques to help develop a temperature-control device in a chemical plant
- Preparing a series of experiments using electronic devices in cooperation with a scientist or engineer

# Electronics Engineers

Engineering differs from engineering technology in that it tends to be based more extensively on theoretical concepts. Engineers must consider why things happen and then use their background to solve problems, design systems, and perform other broad-based functions.

Electronics engineers conduct research and development activities concerned with the design, manufacture, and testing of electronic components, products, and systems. Their work is vital to the development of products and applications for commercial, industrial, medical, military, and scientific purposes. They may design electrical circuits, electronic components, and integrated systems. They may also fabricate test control apparatuses and equipment, and they may determine procedures for testing products.

Other duties described by the Department of Labor include the following.

> Develops new applications of electrical and dielectric properties in materials used in components, products, or systems. May develop field operation and maintenance of electronic installations. May evaluate systems and recommend modifications to eliminate malfunctions or changes in system requirements. May specialize in development of electronic principles and technology in fields such as telecommunications, aerospace guidance, acoustics, industrial controls and measurements, laboratory techniques, computers, electronic data processing and reduction, teaching aids and techniques, radiation detection, and biomedical research.

Typical tasks undertaken by an electronics engineer might include:

- Designing new electronic devices such as computer components or medical monitoring equipment

- Adapting or improving components of an existing device (for example, an airplane's autopilot unit)
- Working as a member of a team to design a complex system such as a robot control system
- Writing computer software needed for use of electronic equipment
- Testing equipment (for example, an automated device used to control an assembly line) to assess capabilities or deficiencies
- Establishing performance standards for electronic equipment
- Developing maintenance schedules for electronic devices and systems
- Analyzing and solving problems in equipment operation
- Estimating the cost of work to be performed
- Supervising technicians and other technical personnel
- Seeing that safety standards are met in use or production of electronic equipment
- Completing research or production reports

## Places of Employment

Electronics engineers and engineering technologists enjoy a great deal of diversity in the types of jobs available. They are employed by a wide range of companies and organizations. Examples include engineering consulting firms, computer manufacturers, research and development firms, utility companies, manufacturers of electronic equipment, and many others. In addition, some work for government agencies ranging from the National Aeronautics and Space Administration (NASA) to the U.S. Department of Energy, as well as in the military.

The biggest proportion of jobs can be found in large and medium-sized cities, but jobs can be found across the United States and Canada and in other countries around the world.

## Working Environment

Like others following electronics careers, persons employed as engineers and engineering technologists often work in comfortable surroundings. Some engineers have their own private offices, and even those who work within cubicles or other shared work spaces tend to enjoy relatively pleasant work environments.

In some cases, significant travel may be involved. An engineer employed for a large corporation, for example, may travel to plants or worksites around the country or even internationally. This can be an interesting experience for those who enjoy seeing new places.

## Educational Preparation

Completion of a college-level program is a must to prepare for employment in this area. The level of studies varies. For those in electronics engineering technology, subjects studied are somewhat similar to those noted in previous chapters, but with more math and physics as a basic requirement. At Mesa Community College in Mesa, Arizona, for example, students must meet an algebra requirement before beginning the electronics engineering technology program. For this purpose, most enroll in a special course called Beginning Algebra for Technology. They then complete the following required courses:

Engineering Analysis Tools and Techniques
Engineering Problem Solving and Design
Circuit Analysis I
Circuit Analysis II
Solid-State Devices and Circuits I
Digital Logic and Circuits
Computer Programming for Technology
Solid-State Devices and Circuits II
Microprocessor Concepts
College Algebra and Functions
Plane Trigonometry
Calculus with Analytic Geometry I
Calculus with Analytic Geometry II
General Physics I
General Physics or Fundamental Chemistry and Lab

In addition, students complete a number of courses in general studies:

First Year Composition (two courses)
Oral Communication (Introduction to Human
    Communication or Public Speaking or Small Group
    Communication)
Critical Reading (Critical and Evaluative Reading or
    equivalent by assessment)
Humanities/Social Science (one course in the Humanities
    and Fine Arts and one course in the Social and
    Behavioral Science area)

These courses provide a broad background in basic electronics concepts as well as the general education required as a portion of a college education. Students learn both mathematical and scientific theory and hands-on application of engineering technology principles.

For students studying engineering, even more intensive preparation is required. The typical bachelor's level engineering program includes a healthy number of courses in physics (with more emphasis on calculus than in engineering technology programs), math, computer science, specialized engineering courses, and additional general studies requirements. Some programs are so demanding, in fact, that they require five years to complete instead of four.

This is not to indicate that engineering is unreasonably difficult, but anyone planning on such a career should understand that it is considered one of the more challenging areas college students can take. If you are interested, go for it! But be sure to weigh the challenges and advantages of this area against other careers in electronics before going ahead.

## Employment Outlook

The U.S. Department of Labor projects that job growth for electronics engineers may reach between 9 and 17 percent for the decade ending in 2014. Similar job growth is anticipated for electronics engineering technicians. For both career areas, many job openings will come about through employment growth. Other positions will become available as current workers retire or take other jobs.

# 6

# SPECIALIZED ELECTRONICS OCCUPATIONS

SOME JOBS IN electronics require similar skills and training as those described in previous chapters but differ in that they involve work that is specialized to one industry or type of electronic equipment. Following is a brief overview of some of these job categories.

## Broadcast Technicians

The specialized nature of the radio and television industries requires technicians to operate and maintain the equipment used for recording and transmitting information. Broadcast technicians fill this role by working with equipment such as television cameras, transmitters, microphones, audiotape recorders, videotape recorders, and other electronic devices.

Technicians in this field hold a variety of job titles. Examples include:

- Audio control engineer
- Recording engineer
- Video control engineer
- Field technician
- Maintenance technician
- Transmitter operator

In many cases, the term *engineer* in this area is used as a synonym for *technician* and does not necessarily require a college degree in engineering. Instead, training at a vocational school or two-year college often will suffice.

## Work Performed

Typical jobs that are performed by broadcast technicians include the following.

- Operating equipment in a booth or control room during a television broadcast
- Setting up, operating, and dismantling equipment used for a remote-site radio broadcast
- Operating transmitters and maintaining broadcast logs
- Servicing and repairing electronic broadcasting equipment
- Operating sound, lighting, or special effects equipment

## Places of Employment

Broadcast technicians work at radio and television stations throughout North America. Most such facilities are located in or near cities, although not all stations are restricted to large metropolitan areas (especially with radio). Some jobs also can be found with universities, corporations, or other organizations that produce training materials, DVDs, or other broadcast-type materials.

### Working Environment

A special advantage experienced by many broadcast technicians is the sense of glamour that often accompanies radio and television work. For example, a technician who assists a television news crew may be exposed to a variety of newsworthy events or encounter famous people. The excitement of working as part of a team striving for high-quality broadcasting also can prove stimulating.

## Computer Service Technicians

In the last few decades, computers have become an increasingly vital part of life, not just in high-technology industries, but also in daily life. Almost every company or organization uses computers, accomplishing tasks ranging from word processing and e-mail communication to control of manufacturing processes or electronic fulfillment of merchandise orders. This means that demand exists for persons who can maintain and repair computer equipment.

Computer service technicians hold jobs with firms that sell computers, with companies and large organizations that own large numbers of computers and choose to employ their own service personnel, and with the military. They service and repair computers and related equipment such as printers and data storage devices.

### Work Performed

Examples of work performed by computer service technicians include:

- Installing computers and computer systems, including hooking up electrical connections and testing equipment before it is used
- Running diagnostic programs and identifying equipment malfunctions
- Replacing components of computers and related equipment
- Cleaning and adjusting equipment such as disk drives, printers, and other components and peripherals
- Transporting computer equipment to and from a central repair shop
- Calling on customers and maintaining positive relationships with them

## *Educational Background*

The background required for working in this area is much like that needed for other technicians providing service and repair functions. Of course, special emphasis on computers and how they work is a prime component of any preparation for a career in this area.

## *Working Conditions*

One difference between this field and some related areas is that more night or weekend work may be required, at least with some employers. Because computers are so important to the operations of many businesses, malfunctions may require immediate attention. This can mean being on call during night or weekend hours, or, in some cases, putting in shift work.

A plus in such situations may be the opportunity to earn extra income, which is often paid at an overtime rate of one and one-half to two times the normal hourly wage.

# Employment Outlook

Due in part to the increasing reliability of computer equipment, job growth in this area has diminished somewhat in the last few years, and overall employment of computer service technicians is expected to grow more slowly than the average for all occupations during the period ending in 2014, according to the U.S. Department of Labor. This means that growth of up to 8 percent may occur. For jobs in the broadcast industry, employment is expected to decline. Even in areas where job growth is limited, however, the need to replace workers who transfer to other occupations or leave the labor force for other reasons will result in significant numbers of job openings.

In general, job opportunities related to broadcasting or computer service should be best for applicants with related postsecondary training. Prospects will also vary depending on geographical location and the condition of the local or national economy, among other factors.

# Related Occupations

Persons who enjoy working with electronic devices may apply such skills in a variety of other job categories. These include:

- Communications equipment mechanics
- Elevator installers and repairers
- Home appliance and power-tool repairers
- Office machine and cash register servicers
- Telephone installers
- Vending machine servicers and repairers

Job demands, training, and other factors of careers in these fields are similar to those discussed in previous chapters and will not be repeated here. A general background in electronics can provide the basis for branching off into one of these specialty areas.

Another potential job category is that of manager. Technicians or engineers may move into supervisory roles because in many organizations managers are needed to supervise the work of staff.

An interesting program is offered by Southern Illinois University in Carbondale, Illinois. SIU's bachelor of science degree in electronics systems technologies is designed for graduates of associate degree programs in electronics who would like to pursue a long-term career in the electronics industry. The program offers students a chance to combine technical and managerial skills.

Students in this program take courses in both electronics and management. The program also includes a general education requirement. Students who have developed specialties in military service (such as radar, ground equipment electronics systems, communications, navigation, and avionic instruments) may build upon their experiences.

Students pursuing this degree option select from the following programs of study.

- **Biomedical instrumentation technology.** Emphasizing repairing, installing, selling, and managing technology within the medical industry
- **Industrial electronics technology.** Repairing, installing, selling, and managing technology associated with robotic and industrial control systems

- **Communications technology.** Repairing, installing, selling, and managing technology associated with telephone systems, wireless communication, video, and audio equipment
- **Microcomputer technology.** Repairing or installing microprocessor-based equipment

In addition to the major areas of employment in electronics, other career areas may include working with electronic devices or principles. For example, automobile technicians working with contemporary cars and trucks may deal with electronic components and testing devices. The same is true for aircraft mechanics (particularly those who specialize in avionics), various types of engineers, physicists, and many others.

The overall outlook is that for persons interested in electronics, plenty of career options are available. The employment possibilities in this area are varied indeed!

# 7

---

# EDUCATIONAL OPTIONS

IF YOU ELECT to pursue a career in electronics, you'll most likely need to complete a special training or educational program. While some limited possibilities may exist for self-taught workers, most employers expect job applicants to have acquired specialized knowledge through a structured training program.

Approaches to achieving this knowledge vary. For some jobs at the technician's level, on-the-job training is a possibility. But for the majority of jobs in electronics, the best approach begins with completing an electronics program offered by a school or college. Following such a path involves planning ahead, selecting the right program and institution, and then completing each course required to earn a diploma, certificate, degree, or other credential.

## Making Educational Plans

To succeed with any educational effort, it's best to plan ahead in as much detail as possible. Students who make their decisions about education at the last moment often encounter all kinds of difficulties. In fact, educators agree that those who enroll late are much more likely to fail or drop out than are most other students.

In advance planning, consider such facts as the following.

- Types of schools offering electronics programs
- Location of schools in relation to your home (for example, is a given school within reasonable commuting distance, or will it be necessary for you to live in a dormitory or apartment?)
- Options for completing courses online or via other distance learning approaches
- Level of educational offerings provided (for example, bachelor's degree, associate degree, or certificate)
- Length of time required in order to complete the program
- Cost
- Availability of financial aid, if needed
- Application deadlines
- Prerequisites (courses or skills needed before you can be admitted to a given school, its electronics program, or individual courses)
- Your own abilities to complete the required work

To plan ahead, you will need to gather information, ask questions, and make decisions. It is important to realize that any efforts you make to complete a training or educational program can pay off for years to come, so be sure to approach this matter with the seriousness it deserves.

# Reviewing Educational Options

How do you select the right school or college to obtain an appropriate educational background in electronics? A good first step is taking some time to review basic information about the school in general and specifically about its electronics program (or programs, if more than one is offered).

Don't make the mistake of assuming that all schools or programs are the same, for they may have huge differences. Just because a school is close at hand, for instance, doesn't necessarily mean it is the best choice for you. Or the fact that a representative tries to get you to enroll may not be sufficient reason to choose the program being touted (after all, that is the job of men and women who recruit for colleges and schools). The truth is, schools vary in price, quality, level of instruction, effectiveness in placing graduates in good jobs, and many other factors.

In selecting a school, first make sure it is the right kind of institution for your goals. For example, if you want to work in the repair area, a trade school or vocational school may provide sufficient training. But what if you plan to pursue electronic engineering technology? In most such cases, only a postsecondary institution such as a community or technical college will suffice. For engineering, you will need to attend a four-year school.

Your choices in types of schools may include the following.

- Vocational schools at the secondary (high school) level
- Trade or technical schools
- Two-year colleges
- Four-year colleges and universities

## *Vocational Schools*

If you have not yet finished high school, you may be able to take classes in electronics at your high school or at a nearby school that has been designated as a provider of vocational training for your area. Vocational courses in electronics usually do not offer as much detail at this level as at the postsecondary level, but they can get you started.

If you have already completed school, or if you dropped out without finishing, you may be able to enroll in an adult education program run by a local public school district or vocational school. Such programs often are offered at night to accommodate adults who have other jobs but would like to attain the skills to make a career change. Usually, no special background is needed to qualify for such courses, and they may be offered at low cost or even free of charge.

## *Trade Schools*

Trade schools may be called proprietary schools, technical schools, institutes, or even business, career, or technical colleges, although they are not really colleges in the true sense of the word. Their main purpose is to offer short-term occupational training. Some schools may specialize in just one area. For example, some specialize entirely in electronics training. Others offer a variety of programs in different career fields. See Appendix A for a partial listing of trade and technical schools offering electronics programs.

A distinctive feature of trade schools is that they concentrate on the major subject to a greater degree than colleges, and sometimes they focus exclusively on the subject. Students who study electronics at a trade school may not be required to take nontechnical courses such as English composition, literature, history, or psychology. This may be seen as an advantage by some students, especially those who have not enjoyed going to school in the past. Not only can other courses be avoided, but the lack of them can speed up the process of completing a training program. In many cases, such a program can be completed in months rather than years.

Of course, life is full of trade-offs, and this is one area where such differences can be substantial. Be sure to keep in mind the following facts as you consider trade schools versus other types of training opportunities.

1. **Courses are not usually transferable.** This means that if you decide later to go to college, the classes you completed in trade school will not count for college credits. You may have to start over.

2. **Trade schools may be expensive.** Most of these schools operate as businesses. Unlike other schools that may be subsidized by the government or run on a nonprofit basis, they must make a profit to survive. Thus, fees may be very high compared to public two-year colleges.

An offsetting factor is that financial aid awards may be correspondingly higher, canceling out much of the difference in terms of what you actually pay out of your own pocket. But if part of your financial aid is based on loans, you will be paying back a substantial amount of money over a long period of time. You can be liable for such a loan even if you drop out of school and change your mind about a career in electronics.

3. **Reputations vary.** Some trade schools have earned excellent reputations among students, companies that employ graduates, and the local communities they serve. But some others are not well regarded, and employers may be less than enthusiastic about hiring their graduates. Because the trade school's ultimate goal is to make a profit, educational quality can sometimes be sacrificed.

This is not to say that you will receive ineffective training at a trade school, but it is best to check out factors related to quality. Some schools advertise that they are registered, certified, or approved by the state or other government agencies, but this often means little more than the payment of a licensing fee and has nothing to do with quality. A better indicator is accreditation by an organization such as the Accrediting Commission of Career Schools and Colleges of Technology. This accreditation should be indicated in school publications; if it is not, chances are the school has not earned such a designation.

## Two-Year Colleges

Another option for preparing for a career in electronics is to enroll in a two-year college, which may be called a junior, community, or technical college (see Appendix B for a partial list of two-year colleges offering electronics programs). Many such colleges offer a choice between (1) a basic program that can be completed in a year or less and (2) an associate degree program that normally takes two years as a full-time student to complete. The former may be much like programs offered by trade schools, with the advantage that the two-year college tends to be much less expensive.

Associate degree programs take longer to finish because students must take classes not just in electronics, but also in other subjects. For example, you might study English composition or technical writing, history, physical education, or sociology. Only a few such classes must be completed, but they are a requirement to earn a two-year college degree.

Another consideration is that many courses completed at two-year colleges can be transferred to four-year colleges and universities. This may or not be in your plans at first, but educational goals often change. Earning credits that can be transferred may be to your advantage in the future. It is important to remember that courses completed at trade schools, by comparison, rarely will be accepted for credit by colleges and universities.

If short-term training leading to a job in electronics is your only goal, you may opt for a program offered by a two-year college that leads to a diploma or certificate instead of a degree. In this case, courses may not be designed for transfer, and you may not need to take courses in general studies. Instead, you will study electronics and closely related subjects exclusively. If such a program is available at a nearby community or technical college, you may find it much more affordable than a trade school.

## *Four-Year Schools*

Four-year colleges and universities usually do not offer programs to train technicians, although some four-year schools have community college components or other offerings in this area. But if you want a degree in engineering, a college or university is the only option.

Many large universities and a number of smaller four-year colleges offer programs in electronics engineering or a related area. A few offer four-year programs in engineering technology, although these are not as common.

Many colleges specialize in certain areas (such as the liberal arts) and as a result do not offer engineering programs. To find out if a program is available at any given college or university, consult the college catalog or the admissions office. If you are interested in programs beyond the bachelor's degree, check with the graduate school at any university in which you are potentially interested.

Unlike community colleges, most four-year schools do not practice open admissions. You must meet certain admission requirements, and many schools operate on a competitive basis and accept only a limited number of applicants. Before pursuing a four-year college, be sure to find out how the school admits students, what kind of information is required, and when it must be submitted. Typical requirements include ACT or SAT scores—the higher, the better—and a transcript of your high school courses and grades.

## Choosing a School or College

Consider the following as you decide what educational path would be best for you to follow.

### *Four-Year Universities and Colleges*

If you are interested in pursuing a degree from a four-year university or college, take the following steps.

1. **Make sure you know at what level programs are offered.** As previously mentioned, just because a school calls itself a college does not necessarily mean it really operates on the collegiate level. To make certain, examine the school's catalog or website to see whether students earn diplomas, certificates, or associate degrees. Look also at information on transfer programs (if any), relationships with other schools (such as membership in a state community college system), and other basic details.

2. **Consult the catalog for other information.** In reviewing a catalog, take time also to review any sections on electronics programs or courses. Watch for details such as:

- The kinds of jobs graduates are prepared to perform
- How many courses must be completed

- Length of time to complete a program
- Descriptions of electronics courses
- Accreditation (If none is listed, beware. Colleges should be accredited by a regional accrediting group such as the North Central Association of Colleges and Schools, the Southern Association of Colleges and Schools, or the New England Association of Colleges and Schools.)
- Admission requirements
- Credentials of faculty

3. **Visit the school.** Even if a school you are considering is not a local one, be sure to visit the campus. Enrolling sight unseen can lead to problems. Take a look at electronics labs, classrooms, and other points of interest. Some schools that sound great in their promotional materials are much less attractive in real life, and they may not have the up-to-date equipment a program in electronics should offer. If possible, always take a look for yourself before making a decision about any school.

4. **Ask questions.** What is the school's placement rate for those who have completed programs in electronics? How is it viewed in the community? How do former students feel about it? Does it have a good reputation? Pose questions such as these to school officials, older friends, local businesspeople, or others who may be in a position to know about the school. Such information can be valuable in making an informed choice.

5. **Consider costs.** In making your selection, a major factor should be the cost of attending. Unless money is no issue with you and your family, it pays to look closely at this matter.

Costs for tuition, fees, and other expenses vary widely from one school to another. In general, the least expensive schools are those considered public institutions because they are funded through tax revenues. For example, public school systems—including not only elementary and secondary education, but also many vocational schools and adult education programs—often offer free or low-cost classes to anyone who can benefit.

## Public Two-Year Colleges

The least expensive of the schools that assess tuition tend to be public two-year colleges. Most community, junior, and technical colleges attempt to keep costs as low as possible so that almost anyone can attend. Many two-year colleges charge less than $2,500 for a full academic year. This is very inexpensive when compared with the tuition charged by the typical college or university. In addition, almost all community colleges offer financial aid programs for those who can demonstrate financial need.

## Private Schools

It usually costs much more to attend privately owned trade schools and private two-year colleges. Their costs may be much higher than public institutions because they do not receive operating funds from state or local governments. Instead, private schools must rely more on income from tuition and fees charged to students. At trade schools or private colleges, even a short-term program in electronics may cost thousands of dollars to complete. From a dollars-and-cents viewpoint, a public school may make the best choice unless an electronics program is not available in a public school in your area or you believe a private school's quality and reputation are worth the extra investment.

Private schools do enjoy the advantage that their students may receive larger amounts of student aid than those at public institutions. Federal student aid programs calculate awards in part on the cost of attending a given school, meaning that higher aid packages may offset some of the high costs of private schools. Some of these awards may come in the form of loans, however, and they must be paid back over a period of years. So be sure to analyze all related cost factors before enrolling at any school, even if financial aid is available.

## Types of Expenses

Expenses that have to be paid can include some or even all of the following.

- **Tuition.** May be assessed as a lump sum, a certain amount for each class or each credit hour, or in some other way
- **Fees.** May be a synonym for tuition or may apply to other costs
- **Application fees.** Often required before enrollment and usually nonrefundable, even if you decide not to attend
- **Book costs.** Not usually charged along with tuition, but they represent an extra cost students must pay, usually to the school's bookstore; may be several hundred dollars for a single term
- **Lab fees.** Often charged to help cover the cost of equipment and supplies
- **Activity fees.** May be charged even for students who do not participate in recreational or cultural activities
- **Health fees.** Special fees that may be charged to support student health services for all students
- **Room and board.** May be charged directly by the school or may consist of costs to live off campus

- **Commuting expenses.** For students who live at home and commute; can include gasoline, car upkeep, parking fees, bus or train fare, or other expenses
- **Other fees.** May include costs for taking special tests, technology fees, having transcripts sent to employers or other schools, dropping or adding classes, or other purposes

By far, the greatest expense is for tuition and basic fees, but it is important not to overlook other costs in making educational plans.

## Getting Financial Aid

Studying electronics can be expensive, but students who need financial help usually can obtain it. If money is a problem, you could consider applying for financial aid. This can come in the form of a grant, scholarship, loan, work-study award, or other financial assistance.

For most students interested in electronics courses, the best source of aid is the U.S. government. Every year, millions of students receive money from the government through a variety of financial aid programs. Other programs for loans, grants, or scholarships are sponsored at the state level.

To obtain student aid through most government programs, it is necessary to show financial need. The needier you are, the more funding you can expect. At the same time, persons who need help but are not as disadvantaged can qualify for special loans offered at low interest rates.

Other sources of aid include schools and colleges themselves. Many offer a variety of financial aid awards including scholarships, loans, and grants. Also, thousands of private organizations sponsor special aid programs ranging from scholarships to grants.

Students in electronics and other fields will find that a great deal of financial aid is available. The key is to be aggressive in pursuing such assistance. For those willing to fill out forms, meet deadlines, and provide the needed information, chances of receiving financial aid are excellent.

## *Applying for Aid*

The first step in obtaining student aid from the government is to provide information about your family's income, assets, debts, and other financial matters. This is done by completing a detailed application form called the Free Application for Federal Student Aid (FAFSA). You may submit an FAFSA:

- Through the Internet by using FAFSA on the Web
- By using FAFSA Express software, a free software program
- By having your school submit your application electronically
- By mailing a paper FAFSA

You can get a paper FAFSA from your high school or postsecondary school. For faster results, fill out a copy online.

For more information, contact:

Federal Student Aid Information Center
P.O. Box 84
Washington, DC 20044
www.studentaid.gov

You can also obtain these and related forms from high school guidance counselors and from financial aid offices in colleges and trade schools. If you are unsure which form is best for your situation, check with a counselor or financial aid officer.

At first the forms might seem too demanding or even an invasion of privacy, but go ahead and fill one out. If successful, your efforts can lead to a grant, loan, or other assistance worth thousands of dollars.

In this process, make certain you meet the application deadlines. The best time to apply is around January 1 of the calendar year in which you plan to begin your fall postsecondary studies. In other words, this will be eight or nine months before you begin school. Because some federal programs award money on a first-come, first-served basis, the earlier you can submit your application, the better. At any rate, make certain that you apply before May 1 for fall enrollment.

## Financial Aid Publication

A new government publication beginning in 2006–2007 is *Funding Education Beyond High School: The Guide to Federal Student Aid.* This publication combines and updates the information previously contained in *The Student Guide* and in *Funding Your Education*, which are no longer being published. This comprehensive reference guide includes an overview of the financial aid process and detailed tips on undertaking each phase of the application process. A glossary clarifying financial aid terminology is also included. This guide is available free at www.studentaid.gov.

## Types of Financial Aid Available

The government sponsors several types of aid programs. Following is a brief overview of major awards available. Keep in mind that many students receive a package of aid consisting of several different types of awards.

## Pell Grants

Pell Grants are designed for students who have genuine financial need. Many people consider them the most desirable type of award available. After all, a grant does not have to be repaid—ever!

The amount any one student receives will vary according to individual finances, costs at the school being attended, and related factors. Recent students have received anywhere from a few hundred dollars to well over $2,000 yearly. This award is based on need, not grades or other academic factors.

The major appeal of this type of grant is that if you really need one, you are almost certain to receive it if you apply properly. This means that financial limitations should not keep you from pursuing a career in electronics.

## Supplemental Educational Opportunity Grants

Supplemental Educational Opportunity Grants (SEOG) are much like Pell Grants, but not as many awards are available each year. They, too, need not be repaid. Because overall funds are limited, it is important to apply early if you hope to land one of these grants.

## Loan Options

Government-sponsored loan programs provide another set of options. Some are offered by the government itself, while others come from private lending agencies with government backing. They must be repaid after your education is completed, but most offer a long time to repay as well as lower interest rates than ordinary commercial loans.

One of the most popular loan programs is the Perkins Loan program. This provides loans with relatively low interest rates and plenty of time to repay the loan.

Another widely used program is the Stafford Loan program, which offers similar benefits. The Stafford is different, however, in that such loans are obtained directly from a bank, credit union, or other financial institution. Interest rates are lower than conventional loans thanks to government backing of the loans.

Other loans that place less emphasis on financial need also are available. Many families have incomes that are too high for need-based programs, but a loan still would be helpful in meeting educational expenses. For such situations, both the Parent Loans for Undergraduate Students (PLUS) and the Supplemental Loans for Students (SLS) offer an attractive alternative. PLUS loans are made directly to parents of students, while SLS are taken out by students. Both loans are made through banks or other private lenders, and the major requirement is a good credit rating.

## Work-Study

Some students earn money to apply to school expenses through a college work-study program, where students hold part-time jobs at their college or a cooperating agency. Typical jobs include working in a dean's office, staffing the switchboard, serving as a lab assistant, or helping out in the college's library, bookstore, or grounds crew.

Participants in this program earn at least the federal minimum wage. They also gain job experience, which can be helpful in showing prospective employers that they have been successful workers, as well as the chance to receive letters of recommendation from college staff members who have served as work-study supervisors.

## Additional Aid Possibilities

Other sources of student aid may be available in addition to those offered by the government. For example, consider the following.

- Scholarships and grants offered by individual schools
- Grants or scholarships offered by professional associations related to electronics
- Scholarships sponsored by organizations to which you or a parent belongs, such as churches or civic clubs
- Tuition programs sponsored by companies for their employees (a great possibility if you can gain employment before completing an educational program or wish to move up from one level to another)

# Alternative Training Programs

In addition to electronics programs offered by schools and colleges, other training options also exist. These include apprenticeships, informal on-the-job training, and special training programs offered by employers.

## *Apprenticeship Programs*

One effective way to learn a craft or trade is to serve as an apprentice. This involves working under the guidance of experienced workers in the field being studied.

Apprenticeships represent one of the oldest forms of training in existence. They became common during the Middle Ages, when workers learned the basics of a trade or craft by serving as apprentices to persons with skills gained from years of experience. Although less common today as we benefit from the availability of so many schools, apprenticeships still offer a valid alternative method of training.

Modern apprenticeship programs may be offered by companies, labor unions, or a combination of the two. For electronics technicians, it usually takes three or four years to complete an apprenticeship. An advantage over most other training programs is that participants are paid while they participate. The rate of pay is lower than for fully qualified workers, but it usually is raised as skills are acquired.

Serving as an apprentice is a time-honored tradition. It offers a detailed, methodical method of learning from experienced workers while gaining and maintaining employment. If you are interested in such an opportunity, check with employers in your area to see if apprenticeships are offered and how you might become involved.

## On-the-Job Training and Company Training Programs

Another approach for learning about electronics is to participate in a company-sponsored training program. Some of these opportunities consist of very informal on-the-job training. Others may include structured classes, which may cover material similar to that taught in schools but usually are condensed over a shorter time period. The main advantages of company programs are that no cost is involved (employees may even be paid to attend) and training can be finished rapidly.

Information about company training programs can be obtained from the personnel office of firms that employ electronics technicians and related workers. Announcements of such opportunities also may appear in newspapers or other publications.

# 8

# SALARIES AND BENEFITS

A CAREER IN electronics can lead to good pay and fringe benefits. The actual amounts vary widely depending on the type of job performed and a number of other factors. But in general, persons employed in this field earn significantly more than unskilled workers and more than many skilled workers employed in nontechnical fields. Following are some examples of salaries and wages that can be expected in this field.

## Salaries

According to the U.S. Department of Labor, full-time electronic equipment repairers had a median annual income of more than $42,000 in 2004. This meant that half earned above this amount and half earned less. The top salaries exceeded $60,000 per year. Those employed by the federal government earned median salaries of slightly less than $50,000.

Other annual income figures reported by the Department of Labor include the following (all based on 2004 data):

*Electronic Home Entertainment Equipment Installers and Repairers*
Median: $27,955
Top 10 percent: more than $44,400

*Computer, Automated Teller, and Office Machine Repairers*
Median: $35,152
Top 10 percent: more than $54,662

*Electrical and Electronics Engineering Technicians*
Median: $46,310
Top 10 percent: more than $67,900

Beginning wages vary widely depending on the employer, the region of the country, and other factors. Experienced technicians may earn significantly higher wages than newcomers to the field.

Engineers working in electronics earn even higher salaries. According to the U.S. Department of Labor, most electronics engineers earned between $49,000 and $112,000 in 2005.

It is important to note that wages and salaries vary not only from one type of job to another, but within similar job categories. A number of factors can influence pay levels, including:

• **Educational level.** In general, positions requiring a greater level of educational preparation pay higher salaries. An engineer with a bachelor's or master's degree, for instance, usually will earn more than a technician with two years or fewer of postsecondary training.

• **Location.** Workers in large cities tend to make more than those in rural areas, and those in areas with a higher cost of living usually earn higher wages. For example, housing, food, and other fundamentals tend to cost much more in San Francisco or Baltimore than in rural Mississippi or North Dakota. Thus workers in all categories, including electronics, usually demand correspondingly higher salaries and wages.

• **Economic trends.** During times of inflation, salaries and wages tend to go up. When the regional or national economy slows down, on the other hand, raises may be smaller or nonexistent for a while.

• **Skill and experience.** An experienced technician or other electronics worker generally earns more than one with little or no experience. This is the case in union environments, where apprentices or other new workers must strive to achieve journeyman status. Things might not be as extensively formalized in nonunion settings, but here, too, experienced workers tend to earn more.

• **Job competition.** Competition among companies that employ workers in electronics is often a factor in earning potential. For example, if one firm raises its salaries, another employer in the same city may feel compelled to do the same to avoid having workers leave for better paying jobs. On the other hand, a lack of such competition may help keep salaries at a lower-than-average level.

• **Employer status.** A new business that is struggling to establish itself may not be able to pay as well as one that has flourished for years. Similarly, one that hires only union members may have a higher wage scale than a nonunion operation.

## Benefits

Along with salaries or wages, most employers provide several types of benefits to their employees. Benefits vary from one company to another and are usually more extensive for full-time employees than for part-timers. In some cases, the total amount paid in benefits can be more than 30 percent of the base salary. This can be a significant factor in making a decision about whether to accept a job offer.

Such benefits may include the following.

- Health insurance
- Retirement funds
- Paid sick leave
- Paid vacations
- Worker's compensation in case of injury
- Social Security benefits

In addition, employees in some companies enjoy the added benefit of participating in profit-sharing programs, where they may own stock in the company or obtain bonuses based on the company's overall performance. Other possible benefits include extra medical coverage (such as dental or optical insurance), life insurance, performance bonuses, tuition reimbursements, and others.

In considering any employment situation, it is important to learn what benefits are available before making a decision to accept the job. The total package of salary or wages and fringe benefits should be reviewed when considering one job against another, not just earnings alone.

# 9

## ELECTRONICS ORGANIZATIONS AND CERTIFICATIONS

A COMMON STEREOTYPE in the movies and on television is that of the basement inventor, who labors alone on special projects accompanied by flashing lights, various electronic devices, and other esoteric trappings. But few people in engineering or other technological jobs actually work in isolation. Most men and women who work in electronics coordinate their activities closely with others who perform similar functions. In addition to cooperating in the workplace, many hold membership in special groups related to their professional interests. Such organizations include labor unions, professional societies focusing on different areas of electronics, and other organizations.

## Benefits of Memberships

Participation in an electronics organization can be highly worthwhile. The benefits provided to members range from the sharing of useful information to the sponsorship of special programs to certify technical competency.

### *Electronics Technicians Association, International*

The Electronics Technicians Association, International (ETA) has offered the following reasons why technicians should find membership beneficial.

- Improvement of pay and prestige through group efforts
- Monthly information on various phases of electronics, including circuit descriptions and short quizzes
- Business seminars and other management information for those who are service managers
- Discounts on trade magazines, technical books, and other items
- Opportunities for people with common interests to get together and share information
- A certification program

This association, based in Greencastle, Indiana, welcomes memberships from individual technicians, electronics students, and owners of businesses and institutions, among others. In addition to regular ETA membership, each member may participate in one of the following divisions:

- Educators
- Certified technicians
- Canadian technicians
- Communication technicians
- Medical personnel
- Industrial personnel
- Shop owners

For more information, contact ETA at:

ETA, International
5 Depot Street
Greencastle, Indiana 46135
www.eta-i.org

## *International Society of Certified Electronics Technicians*

A similar organization is the International Society of Certified Electronics Technicians, headquartered in Ft. Worth, Texas. Its functions include the direction and administration of:

- The Certified Electronics Technician (CET) program
- A national apprenticeship and training program
- Technical information training and upgrading programs
- Serviceability inspection programs

This association originated as an offshoot of the National Electronic Association in 1970. To be eligible for membership, an electronics technician must have passed the organization's CET exam.

Once membership is conferred, men and women benefit from not only the information and networking provided, but also the stature of having passed a recognized certification process.

For more information, contact the society directly at:

International Society of Certified Electronics Technicians
3608 Pershing Avenue
Fort Worth, Texas 76107
www.iscet.org

## Association of Communications and Electronics Schools International

Another helpful organization is the Association of Communications and Electronics Schools International (ACES). This is a not-for-profit worldwide certification and testing organization. It provides a number of training and certification programs. Special features of this organization include "hands-on" skills testing along with written certification examinations, tool and equipment standards, and training that is not specific to vendors.

For more details, contact ACES International at:

ACES International
5241 Princess Anne Road
Virginia Beach, Virginia 23462
www.acesinternational.org

## Other Organizations

Those employed in electronics jobs other than as technicians may elect to participate in other organizations. Owners of their own electronics repair firms, for example, may join a group such as the

National Electronic Sales and Service Dealers Association. Engineers may join an organization for engineers from a variety of fields, or they may join one that is more specialized, such as the Institute of Electrical and Electronics Engineers. See Appendix C for a list of more electronics-related organizations.

## Labor Unions

Many persons employed in electronics belong to labor unions. These organizations allow workers to join together to promote the welfare of members of the group, especially in terms of their relations with employers. Unions have been a major force in American and Canadian business and industry for more than a hundred years. A number of advancements—such as shorter workweeks, higher pay, fringe benefits, and expanded worker rights—have resulted from the efforts of labor unions.

Men and women employed in electronics jobs may belong to a number of unions, including the following:

- International Brotherhood of Electrical Workers
- International Union of Electronic, Electrical, Salaried, Machine, and Furniture Workers
- United Electrical, Radio, and Machine Workers of America
- Federation of Westinghouse Independent Salaried Unions

Some of the benefits offered by labor unions include:

- Apprentice training opportunities
- Guaranteed wage levels and other benefits provided by the employer in accordance with contracts negotiated by union representatives

- Voting rights, such as the right to vote for union officials and the right to vote for or against proposed contracts
- Informative publications for members
- Pension plans and other benefits managed by the union for its members
- Protection against unfair labor practices
- Strength in numbers, which helps counterbalance the power employers can hold over their employees

Labor unions depend on dues from members to sustain their operations. This means that as a member, you must pay a specified amount each month or pay period toward these costs. A typical amount for dues is a contribution of the equivalent of two hours' wages per month, although this can vary. For a large union with thousands of members, overall income can be significant. This money is then used to support a wide range of union activities to improve wages, working conditions, and other employment-related matters.

At any given time, a labor union might be lobbying Congress in support of legislation that would have a positive impact on its members, negotiating with employers for a new contract, sponsoring a scholarship program for children of union members, or working to improve members' medical benefits.

In the electronics field, union membership is more common with employees of large firms than it is with smaller companies such as one- or two-person repair businesses. It also is more typical of urban areas than rural ones and in certain geographical locations. The southern United States, for example, is not a strong union region compared to the northern United States and parts of Canada.

In some settings, union membership is virtually required. Elsewhere, it may be entirely up to the individual. In any case, many persons employed in electronics-related jobs find union membership beneficial.

## Certifications

How can you prove to a prospective employer or customer that you are qualified to repair electronic equipment or perform other work in electronics? Holding a diploma or degree in an electronics field is one good indicator of competence. Another is to become certified through a nationally recognized certification process such as that offered by the Electronics Technicians Association, International. It leads to one of the following designations:

- **Associate.** The exam at this level is offered to students and to technicians with fewer than four years of experience.
- **Journeyman.** This level is designed for technicians with at least four years of experience and/or education in electronics. The exam includes the basic electronics information required for associates, as well as an option of the student's choice.
- **Senior.** Requiring eight years of experience, this level also requires a higher passage rate than the journeyman designation.
- **Master.** Technicians with at least eight years of experience who can demonstrate competency in six major electronics categories can earn this level of recognition.

Categories and specialty areas in which students can be tested include the following:

*Category*
Consumer electronics
Video distribution
Telecommunications
Industrial
Computer
Biomedical

*Specialty Areas*
Radio/TV, VCR, sound
MATV, antenna, satellite
Phone, data, microwave, VSAT

Students and technicians take these certification exams at a variety of locations around the United States and Canada, including schools, colleges, and at other locations. Those in the military can sit for the exams at military bases around the world. Upon passing, technicians receive certificates and become registered with the Electronics Technicians Association, International as certified engineering technicians (CETs). This can prove to be valuable in many different ways, ranging from intangible benefits such as increased self-confidence to tangible proof of competencies needed to obtain a job or promotion.

If you plan to work as a technician, taking one or more certification exams is well worth considering. Certification credentials can be a valuable asset for your entire professional life.

# 10

# GETTING STARTED
## IN ELECTRONICS

NOW THAT YOU have reviewed the information provided in previous chapters, does a career in electronics seem to match your own interests and abilities? Can you see yourself working as an electronics technician or engineer or in some other position in the field? If so, the next step is to make concrete plans for pursuing such a career, and then follow up on them.

## Taking the First Steps

Here are seven basic steps you might take to get started in the direction of an electronics career:

1. If you are still in high school, take any related courses that are available. For example, most physics courses provide information needed to understand the basic concepts and theories behind elec-

tronics. If vocational classes are offered, you might complete an introductory electronics class, even if you plan to pursue post-secondary training in the field. That way, you can gain some hands-on experience in working with electronics devices.

2. In addition to high school courses, other kinds of training programs may be available to you. If you are still in high school, don't wait until graduation or late in your senior year to check these out, but try to plan ahead. If you are an adult who has completed—or dropped out of—school, why put things off any longer? Start looking around now for the training that can improve your future.

3. Once you decide what kind of program and school seem best for you (for example, a community college or a trade school), fill out admission applications or any other required forms.

4. Apply for financial aid if you need such assistance.

5. Once you are admitted, go to class, apply yourself, and earn a diploma or degree in an electronics field.

6. If you prefer an alternative approach, apply for a job with a firm that offers its own on-the-job training program or cooperates in offering an apprenticeship program. Then work diligently to complete the program.

7. Remember the importance of credentials. When you gain credentials that indicate you are qualified to work in electronics, you can be on your way to a successful career!

## Landing a Job

The next step after gaining educational credentials is to locate a job for which you are qualified. This may happen quickly and easily, or it may take weeks or months of effort. Because of the demand for workers in electronics, most persons with the right qualifications should have less difficulty in obtaining a job than do those in many other fields. At any rate, the process requires initiative. It is up to you to find out about job vacancies and then pursue them.

## *Identifying Job Vacancies*

Online job sites are a great place to identify job openings. Some examples include:

- Monster.com (www.monster.com)
- Hot Jobs (http://hotjobs.yahoo.com)
- JobWeb (www.jobweb.com)

Another place to locate job openings is in the classified section of any newspaper, although such listings are increasingly being supplemented or replaced by online information. This is particularly true of daily papers serving larger towns and cities.

Following is a representative classified ad that appeared in a major newspaper.

ELECTRONIC TECH. Candidate will be responsible for repair and maintenance of electronic security systems consisting of microprocessor and PLC-based locking control systems, CCTV systems, perimeter security systems, intercom systems, etc. Positions available in several cities. Allow for travel in U.S. Experience in field service or electronic security desired. Will consider recent electronic or EE graduate. An Equal Opportunity Employer.

In addition, companies planning to hire new or replacement workers often post job announcements on bulletin boards or in other public places, as well as on their websites. Any firm's human resources officer or personnel office also will provide this information on request.

Another source of job information is your local employment service or job service office. These offices are supported by state or local governments to provide assistance in locating jobs.

A school or college you have attended also should provide assistance in job searches. To obtain help, contact the school's placement office or career counselor.

Websites of local companies (or companies located elsewhere if you're interested in relocating) often list job openings. Look under "jobs" or "human resources" to find job postings. Unions and professional associations may also provide such listings.

## Filling Out Job Applications

A standard procedure in seeking a job is filling out a written job application. If this is required, be sure to do the following:

1. Take your time in filling out the form.
2. Answer all questions completely and honestly.
3. Be as neat as possible. If time and circumstances allow, type the application. If this is not possible, write neatly and legibly. Use a pen, not a pencil, and remember that you are trying to make a good impression.
4. Check your work closely for errors in spelling or grammar.
5. Prepare a neatly word-processed résumé in advance, and attach it to applications or use it instead of application forms, if allowed.
6. For persons whom you list as references, make certain you have contacted them in advance to get their permission for such usage and to make sure that they will be prepared to give you a positive recommendation.

## *Doing Well in Job Interviews*

If all goes well, a completed application will be followed by a job interview. It is here that most jobs are won or lost, with the written application serving only to get you to this stage. To do your best in interviews, take measures such as these.

1. **Be on time.** Lateness only makes a bad impression, and it may cost you the job.

2. **Avoid being too eager.** Even if you think you need the job badly, try not to show it. A calm, professional manner works best. Act interested, but not desperate.

3. **Dress neatly.** Appearances do count, so make sure you wear clean, neat clothes.

4. **Engage in a two-way conversation.** Although it is the interviewer's job to ask most of the questions, ask some questions of your own. These should dwell on the nature of the job, not on issues such as wages and benefits, which can be discussed in more detail if you are offered the job. Show that you are interested and capable of asking intelligent questions.

Will your interview lead to a job? One never knows in any given situation. But it only takes one success! Then you can begin working in the electronics field, with all the potential such a move holds for a truly interesting career.

# Trade and Technical Schools Offering Electronics Programs

The following private trade and technical schools are just some of those offering instructional programs in electronics. In some cases, schools that offer computer repair are also listed.

Check the yellow pages or websites for schools and locations convenient to you.

## United States

### Alabama

Herzing College of Business and Technology
280 W. Valley Ave.
Homewood, AL 35209
www.herzing.edu

ITT Technical Institute
500 Riverhills Business Park
Birmingham, AL 35242
www.itt-tech.edu

Remington College–Mobile
828 Downtowner Loop W.
Mobile, AL 36609
www.remingtoncollege.edu

## *Arizona*

High Tech Institute
1515 E. Indian School Rd.
Phoenix, AZ 85014
www.hightechinstitute.com

ITT Technical Institute
5005 S. Wendler Dr.
Tempe, AZ 85202
www.itt-tech.edu

ITT Technical Institute
1455 W. River Rd.
Tucson, AZ 85704
www.itt-tech.edu

## *Arkansas*

ITT Technical Institute
4520 S. University
Little Rock, AR 72209
www.itt-tech.edu

## *California*

Advanced Training Associates
1900 Joe Crosson Dr., Ste. C
El Cajon, CA 92020-1236
www.advancedtraining.edu

ITT Technical Institute
2051 Solar Dr.
Oxnard, CA 93036
www.itt-tech.edu

ITT Technical Institute
670 E. Carnegie Dr.
San Bernardino, CA 92408
www.itt-tech.edu

ITT Technical Institute
9680 Granite Ridge Dr.
San Diego, CA 92123
www.itt-tech.edu

ITT Technical Institute
12669 Encinitas Ave.
Sylmar, CA 91342
www.itt-tech.edu

ITT Technical Institute
1530 W. Cameron Ave.
West Corvina, CA 91790
www.itt-tech.edu

Los Angeles ORT Technical Institute
635 S. Harvard Blvd.
Los Angeles, CA 90005
www.laort.com

## Colorado

ITT Technical Institute
500 E. 84th Ave.
Thornton, CO 80229
www.itt-tech.edu

Redstone College
10851 W. 120th Ave.
Broomfield, CO 80021
www.redstonecollege.com

## Connecticut

Connecticut School of Electronics
586 Grasso Blvd.
New Haven, CT 06519
www.ctschoolofelectronics.com

Porter and Chester Institute
138 Weymouth St.
Enfield, CT 06082
www.porterchester.com

## Florida

ITT Technical Institute
7955 NW 12th St.
Miami, FL 33126
www.itt-tech.edu

ITT Technical Institute
4809 Memorial Hwy.
Tampa, FL 33634
www.itt-tech.edu

## Georgia

Career Education Institute
2359 Windy Hill Rd. SE
Marietta, GA 30067-8638
www.ceitraining.com

Career Education Institute
5675 Jimmy Carter Blvd.
Norcross, GA 30071-2965
www.ceitraining.com

## Illinois

Coyne American Institute
330 N. Green St.
Chicago, IL 60607-1300
www.coyneamerican.edu

Coyne American Institute
230 W. Monroe, Ste. 400
Chicago, IL 60607
www.coyneamerican.edu

ITT Technical Institute
1401 Feehanville Dr.
Mount Prospect, IL 60056
www.itt-tech.edu

Lincoln Technical Institute
8317 W. North Ave.
Melrose Park, IL 60160-1605
www.lincolntech.com

## Indiana

ITT Technical Institute
4919 Coldwater Rd.
Fort Wayne, IN 46825
www.itt-tech.edu

ITT Technical Institute
9511 Angola Ct.
Indianapolis, IN 46268
www.itt-tech.edu

## Kentucky

Louisville Technical Institute
3901 Atkinson Square Dr.
Louisville, KY 40218-4528
www.louisvilletech.com

## Louisiana

ITT Technical Institute
140 James Dr. E.
St. Rose, LA 70087
www.itt-tech.edu

## Massachusetts

Career Education Institute
5 Middlesex Ave.
Somerville, MA 02145-1102
www.ceitraining.com

ITT Technical Institute
10 Forbes Rd.
Woburn, MA 01801
www.itt-tech.edu

RETS Technical Center
570 Rutherford Ave.
Charlestown, MA 02129
www.retstech.com

## Michigan

ITT Technical Institute
4020 Sparks Dr. SE
Grand Rapids, MI 49546
www.itt-tech.edu

## *Missouri*

ITT Technical Institute
9150 E. 41st Terr.
Kansas City, MO 64133
www.itt-tech.edu

Vatterott College
927 E. Terra La.
O'Fallon, MO 63366-2748
www.vatterott-college.com

## *Nebraska*

ITT Technical Institute
9814 M St.
Omaha, NE 68127
www.itt-tech.edu

## *New Jersey*

Lincoln Technical Institute
70 McKee Dr.
Mahwah, NJ 07430-2106
www.lincolntech.com

## *New York*

ITT Technical Institute
2295 Millersport Hwy.
Getzville, NY 14068
www.itt-tech.edu

## Ohio

Bryant and Stratton College
1700 E. 13th St.
Cleveland, OH 44114
www.bryantstratton.edu

Total Technical Institute
8720 Brookpart
Brooklyn, OH 44129
www.ttinst.com

## Oklahoma

Spartan College of Aeronautics and Technology
8820 E. Pine St.
Tulsa, OK 74158
www.spartan.edu

## Oregon

ITT Technical Institute
6035 NE 78th Ct.
Portland, OR 97218
www.itt-tech.edu

## Pennsylvania

CHI Institute
520 Street Road
Southampton, PA 18966-3747
www.chitraining.com

Thompson Institute
2593 Philadelphia Ave.
Chambersburg, PA 17201-7904
www.thompson.edu

### Rhode Island

Career Education Institute
622 George Washington Hwy.
Lincoln, RI 02865-4211
www.ceitraining.com

### Tennessee

ITT Technical Institute
2845 Elm Hill Pike
Nashville, TN 37211
www.itt-tech.edu

### Texas

ITT Technical Institute
2101 Waterview Pkwy.
Richardson, TX 75080
www.itt-tech.edu

### Virginia

ITT Technical Institute
863 Glenrock Rd.
Norfolk, VA 23502
www.itt-tech.edu

TESST College of Technology
6315 Bren Mar Dr.
Alexandria, VA 22312-6300
www.kaplan.com

## *Washington*

ITT Technical Institute
12720 Gateway Dr.
Seattle, WA 98168
www.itt-tech.edu

## *Wisconsin*

ITT Technical Institute
6300 W. Layton Ave.
Greenfield, WI 53220
www.itt-tech.edu

# Canada

## *Alberta*

CDI College
805 Manning Rd. NE
Calgary, AB T2E 7M8
www.cdicollege.com

CDI College
8615 51st Ave.
Albrumac Business Centre
Edmonton, AB T6E 6A8
www.cdicollege.com

CDI College
Northgate Centre, Unit 2068
9499 137th Ave. NW
Edmonton, AB T5E 5R8
www.cdicollege.com

Prestwick College
717-7 Ave. SW, Ste. 200
Calgary, AB T2P 0Z3
www.educore.ca

## *British Columbia*

Academy of Learning
32555 Simon Ave., Ste. 300
Abbotsford, BC V2T 4Y2
www.academyoflearning.com

Academy of Learning
200-6446 Nelson Ave.
Burnaby, BC V5H 3J5
www.academyoflearning.com

Academy of Learning
1302 Shopper Row
Campbell River, BC V9W 2E1
www.academyoflearning.com

Academy of Learning
1221 Lonsdale Ave., #300
North Vancouver, BC V7M 2H5
www.academyoflearning.com

Universal Learning Institute
10153 King George Hwy.
Surrey, BC V3T 2W1
www.trainingforjobs.com

## *Manitoba*

CDI College
280 Main St.
Winnipeg, MB R3C 1A9
www.cdicollege.com

Herzing College
723 Portage Ave.
Winnipeg, MB R3G 0M8
www.herzing.edu

## *New Brunswick*

Atlantic Business College
100 Cameron St.
Moncton, NB E1C 5Y6
www.abc.nb.ca

## *Newfoundland and Labrador*

Academy Canada
2 University Dr.
Corner Brook, NL A2H 6E3
www.academycanada.com

Academy Canada
167 Kenmount Rd.
St. John's, NL A1B 3P9
www.academycanada.com

Keyin College
81 LeMarchant St.
Carbonear, NL A1Y 1A9
www.keyin.com

Keyin College
P.O. Box 1327
Marystown, NL A0E 2M0
www.keyin.com

## *Nova Scotia*

Cape Breton Business College
P.O. Box 33
Sydney, NS B1N 3B1
www.cbbc.ns.ca

Centre for Arts and Technology
1467 Brenton St.
Halifax, NS B3J 2K7
www.digitalartschool.com

Success College
800 Sackville Dr.
Lower Sackville, NS B4E 1R8
www.thinksuccess.ca

## *Ontario*

Kingston Learning Centre
52 Abbott St. N., Unit 3
Smiths Falls, ON K7A 1W3
www.kingstonlearningcentre.ca

Metro College of Technology
203 College St., Ste. 201-205
Toronto, ON M5T 1P9
www.metroc.ca

RCC College of Technology
2000 Steeles Ave. W.
Concord, ON L4K 4N1
www.rcc.on.ca

RETS Career Training
2084 Danforth Ave.
Toronto, ON M4C 1J9
www.rets.ca

Toronto College of Technology
265 Yorkland Blvd., Ste. 301
Toronto, ON M2J 1S5
www.torontocollege.com

Westervelt College
1060 Wellington Rd.
London, ON N6E 3W5
www.westerveltcollege.com

# Two-Year Colleges Offering Programs in Electronics

Many two-year colleges offer programs in electronics. Junior, community, and technical colleges can be found throughout the United States and Canada, with most serving a local region from which students commute to classes. Many, but not all, of these colleges offer programs in electronics. Consult any college's catalog or contact its admissions office to find out if electronics programs are available.

A partial list of colleges offering electronics follows. If your local community college is not listed, that does not necessarily mean that it does not offer electronics. For any college in which you are interested, contact the institution directly to make sure.

## *Alabama*

Calhoun Community College
Decatur, AL 35609
www.calhoun.cc.al.us

Gadsden State Community College
Gadsden, AL 35902
www.gadsdenst.cc.al.us

George C. Wallace State Community College
Dothan, AL 36303
www.wallace.edu

Jefferson State Community College
Birmingham, AL 35215
www.jscc.cc.al.us

## *Arizona*

Arizona Western College
Yuma, AZ 85366
www.azwestern.edu

Cochise College
Douglas, AZ 85607
www.cochise.cc.az.us

Eastern Arizona College
Thatcher, AZ 85552
www.eac.edu

Glendale Community College
Glendale, AZ 85302
www.gc.maricopa.edu

Northland Pioneer College
Holbrook, AZ 86025
www.northland.cc.az.us

Phoenix College
Phoenix, AZ 85013
www.pc.maricopa.edu

Pima Community College
Tucson, AZ 85709
www.pima.edu

Rio Salado Community College
Phoenix, AZ 85281
www.rio.maricopa.edu

Yavapai College
Prescott, AZ 86301
www.yc.edu

## *Arkansas*

Arkansas State University–Beebe
Beebe, AR 72012
www.asub.edu

Black River Technical College
Pocahontas, AR 72455
www.blackrivertech.org

East Arkansas Community College
Forrest City, AR 72335
www.eacc.edu

Northwest Arkansas Community College
Bentonville, AR 72712
www.nwacc.edu

Phillips Community College
Helena, AR 72342
www.pccua.edu

## *California*

Cabrillo College
Aptos, CA 95003
www.cabrillo.edu

Chabot College
Hayward, CA 94545
www.chabotcollege.edu

Chaffey College
Rancho Cucamonga, CA 91737
www.chaffey.edu

College of the Redwoods
Eureka, CA 95501
www.redwoods.edu

Cosumnes River College
Sacramento, CA 95823
www.crc.losrios.edu

Fullerton College
Fullerton, CA 92634
www.fullcoll.edu

Golden West College
Huntington Beach, CA 92647
www.gwc.cccd.edu

Los Angeles City College
Los Angeles, CA 90029
www.lacitycollege.edu

Los Angeles Pierce College
Woodland Hills, CA 91371
www.piercecollege.edu

Mission College
Santa Clara, CA 95054
www.mccd.cc.ca.us/mc

Mt. San Antonio College
Walnut, CA 91789
www.mtsac.edu

Mt. San Jacinto College
San Jacinto, CA 92383
www.msjc.cc.ca.us

Napa Valley College
Napa, CA 94558
www.nvc.cc.ca.us

Orange Coast College
Costa Mesa, CA 92626
www.occ.cccd.edu

Rancho Santiago Community College
Santa Ana, CA 92706
www.rsccd.org

Santa Rosa Junior College
Santa Rosa, CA 95401
www.santarosa.edu

Yuba College
Marysville, CA 95901
www.yuba.cc.ca.us

## Colorado

Aims Community College
Greeley, CO 80631
www.aims.edu

Community College of Aurora
Aurora, CO 80011
www.ccaurora.edu

Front Range Community College
Westminster, CO 80030
www.frontrange.edu

Morgan Community College
Ft. Morgan, CO 80701
www.morgancc.edu

Northeastern Junior College
Sterling, CO 80751
www.nejc.cc.co.us

Pikes Peak Community College
Colorado Springs, CO 80906
www.ppcc.edu

Pueblo Community College
Pueblo, CO 81004
www.pueblocc.edu

Red Rocks Community College
Lakewood, CO 80228
www.rrcc.edu

## *Connecticut*

Norwalk Community College
Norwalk, CT 06854
www.nctc.commnet.edu

## *Florida*

Brevard Community College
Cocoa, FL 32922
www.brevard.cc.fl.us

Indian River Community College
Fort Pierce, FL 34981
www.ircc.edu

Lake City Community College
Lake City, FL 32055
www.lakecitycc.edu

Manatee Community College
Bradenton, FL 32406
www.mccfl.edu

Miami Dade College
Miami, FL 33132
www.mdc.edu

Palm Beach Community College
Lake Worth, FL 33461
www.pbcc.cc.fl.us

Santa Fe Community College
Gainesville, FL 32606
www.santafe.cc.fl.us

Seminole Community College
Sanford, FL 32773
www.scc-fl.edu

## *Georgia*

Coastal Georgia Community College
Brunswick, GA 31520
www.cgcc.edu

Gainesville College
Gainesville, GA 30503
www.gc.peachnet.edu

Middle Georgia College
Cochran, GA 31014
www.mgc.edu

## *Hawaii*

University of Hawaii–Hawaii Community College
Hilo, HI 96720
www.hawcc.hawaii.edu

University of Hawaii–Honolulu Community College
Honolulu, HI 96817
www.hcc.hawaii.edu

University of Hawaii–Kauai Community College
Lihue, HI 96766
www.kauaicc.hawaii.edu

## *Idaho*

Eastern Idaho Technical College
Idaho Falls, ID 83404
www.eitc.edu

North Idaho College
Coeur D'Alene, ID 83814
www.nic.edu

## *Illinois*

Black Hawk College
Moline, IL 61265
www.bhc.edu

College of DuPage
Glen Ellyn, IL 60137
www.cod.edu

Elgin Community College
Elgin, IL 60123
www.elgin.edu

Highland Community College
Freeport, IL 61032
www.highland.cc.il.us

Joliet Junior College
Joliet, IL 60431
www.jjc.edu

Kennedy-King College
Chicago, IL 60621
www.ccc.edu/kennedyking

Kishwaukee College
Malta, IL 60150
www.kish.cc.il.us

Lewis and Clark Community College
Godfrey, IL 62035
www.lc.edu

McHenry County College
Crystal Lake, IL 60012
www.mchenry.edu

Moraine Valley Community College
Palos Hills, IL 60465
www.morainevalley.edu

Richard J. Daley College
Chicago, IL 60652
www.daley.ccc.edu

Rock Valley College
Rockford, IL 61114
www.rockvalleycollege.edu

Shawnee Community College
Ullin, IL 62992
www.shawneecc.edu

Southeastern Illinois College
Harrisburg, IL 62946
www.sic.cc.il.us

Triton College
River Grove, IL 60171
www.triton.edu

Wabash Valley College
Mt. Carmel, IL 62863
www.iecc.cc.il.us/wvc

William Rainey Harper College
Palatine, IL 60067
www.harpercollege.edu

## *Iowa*

Clinton Community College
Clinton, IA 52732
www.eicc.edu/general/clinton

Iowa Central Community College
Fort Dodge, IA 50501
www.iccc.cc.ia.us

Iowa Western Community College
Council Bluffs, IA 51503
www.iwcc.cc.ia.us

Kirkwood Community College
Cedar Rapids, IA 52406
www.kirkwood.cc.ia.us

Northwest Iowa Community College
Sheldon, IA 51201
www.nwicc.cc.ia.us

Western Iowa Technical Community College
Sioux City, IA 51102
www.witcc.edu

## Kansas

Allen County Community College
Iola, KS 66749
www.allencc.edu

Butler County Community College
El Dorado, KS 67042
www.butlercc.edu

Cowley County Community College
Arkansas City, KS 67005
www.cowley.cc.ks.us

Garden City Community College
Garden City, KS 67846
www.gcccks.edu

Haskell Indian Nations University
Lawrence, KS 66046
www.haskell.edu/haskell

Johnson County Community College
Overland Park, KS 66210
www.jccc.edu

Kansas City Kansas Community College
Kansas City, KS 66112
www.kckcc.cc.ks.us

Neosho County Community College
Chanute, KS 66720
www.neosho.edu

## *Kentucky*

Big Sandy Community and Technical College
Prestonsburg, KY 41653
www.bigsandy.kctcs.edu

Maysville Community and Technical College
Maysville, KY 41956
www.maysville.kctcs.edu

Owensboro Community and Technical College
Owensboro, KY 42303
www.owensboro.kctcs.edu

Southeast Community and Technical College
Cumberland, KY 40823
www.secc.kctcs.edu

# Maryland

Community College of Baltimore County
Baltimore, MD 21228
www.ccbcmd.edu

Frederick Community College
Frederick, MD 21702
www.frederick.edu

# Massachusetts

Massasoit Community College
Brockton, MA 02402
www.massasoit.mass.edu

Middlesex Community College
Bedford, MA 01730
www.middlesex.mass.edu

# Michigan

Alpena Community College
Alpena, MI 49707
www.alpena.cc.mi.us

Delta College
University Center, MI 48710
www.delta.edu

Gogebic Community College
Ironwood, MI 49938
www.gogebic.edu

Henry Ford Community College
Dearborn, MI 48128
www.hfcc.edu

Kellogg Community College
Battle Creek, MI 49017
www.kellogg.cc.mi.us

Macomb County Community College
Warren, MI 48093
www.macomb.edu

Northwestern Michigan College
Traverse City, MI 49684
www.nmc.edu

Oakland Community College
Bloomfield Hills, MI 48013
www.oaklandcc.edu

Schoolcraft College
Livonia, MI 48152
www.schoolcraft.cc.mi.us

West Shore Community College
Scottville, MI 49454
www.westshore.edu

## *Minnesota*

Anoka-Ramsey Community College
Coon Rapids, MN 55433
www.anokaramsey.edu

North Hennepin Community College
Brooklyn Park, MN 55445
www.nhcc.edu

Rochester Community and Technical College
Rochester, MN 55904-4999
www.rctc.edu

## *Mississippi*

East Central Community College
Decatur, MS 39327
www.eccc.cc.ms.us

Hinds Community College
Raymond, MS 39154
www.hindscc.edu

Holmes Community College
Goodman, MS 39079
www.holmes.cc.ms.us

Itawamba Community College
Fulton, MS 38843
www.icc.cc.ms.us

Jones County Junior College
Ellisville, MS 39437
www.jcjc.cc.ms.us

Mississippi Delta Community College
Moorhead, MS 38761
www.mdcc.cc.ms.us

Mississippi Gulf Coast Community College
Perkinston, MS 39573
www.mgccc.edu

Pearl River Community College
Poplarville, MS 39470
www.prcc.edu

## *Missouri*

East Central College
Union, MO 63084
www.eastcentral.edu

Maple Woods Community College
Kansas City, MO 64156
www.mcckc.edu

Moberly Area College
Moberly, MO 65270
www.macc.cc.mo.us

St. Louis Community College
St. Louis, MO 63102
www.stlcc.edu

## Nebraska

Central Community College, Platte Campus
Columbus, NE 68601
www.cccneb.edu

Mid-Plains Community College
North Platte, NE 69101
www.mpcc.edu

Northeast Community College
Norfolk, NE 68702
www.northeastcollege.com

Western Nebraska Community College
Sidney, NE 69162
www.wncc.net

## Nevada

Truckee Meadows Community College
Reno, NV 89512
www.tmcc.edu

Western Nevada Community College
Carson City, NV 89703
www.wncc.edu

## New Hampshire

New Hampshire Community Technical College
Berlin, NH 03102
www.berlin.nhctc.edu

## New Jersey

Atlantic Cape Community College
Mays Landing, NJ 08330
www.atlantic.edu

Burlington County College
Pemberton, NJ 08068
www.bcc.edu

Mercer County Community College
Trenton, NJ 08690
www.mccc.edu

Union County College
Crawford, NJ 07882
www.ucc.edu

## New Mexico

Eastern New Mexico University–Roswell
Roswell, NM 88202
www.roswell.enmu.edu

New Mexico State University–Carlsbad
Carlsbad, NM 88220
http://artemis.nmsu.edu

## New York

Adirondack Community College
Queensburg, NY 12804
www.sunyacc.edu

Corning Community College
Corning, NY 14830
www.corning-cc.edu

Orange County Community College
Middletown, NY 10940
www.orange.cc.ny.us

Suffolk County Community College
Selden, NY 11784
www.sunysuffolk.edu

## North Carolina

Asheville-Buncombe Technical Community College
Ashville, NC 28801
www.abtech.edu

Catawba Valley Community College
Hickory, NC 28602
www.cvcc.edu

Central Piedmont Community College
Charlotte, NC 28235
www.cpcc.edu

Forsyth Technical Community College
Winston-Salem, NC 27103
www.forsyth.tec.nc.us

Isothermal Community College
Spindale, NC 28160
www.isothermal.edu

Lenoir Community College
Kinston, NC 28502
www.lenoir.cc.nc.us

McDowell Technical Community College
Marion, NC 28752
www.mcdowelltech.cc.nc.us

Sandhills Community College
Pinehurst, NC 28374
www.sandhills.cc.nc.us

Surry Community College
Dobson, NC 27017
www.surry.cc.nc.us

Wilkes Community College
Wilkesboro, NC 28697
www.wilkescc.edu

## Ohio

Columbus State Community College
Columbus, OH 43216
www.cscc.edu

Cuyahoga Community College
Cleveland, OH 44115
www.tri-c.edu

Edison State Community College
Piqua, OH 45356
www.edison.cc.oh.us

Lakeland Community College
Mentor, OH 44060
www.lakeland.cc.oh.us

Stark State College of Technology
Canton, OH 44720
www.starkstate.edu

Washington State College
Marietta, OH 45750
www.wscc.edu

## Oklahoma

Northeastern Oklahoma Agricultural and Mechanical College
Miami, OK 74354
www.neoam.cc.ok.us

Rose State College
Midwest City, OK 73110
www.rose.edu

Tulsa Community College
Tulsa, OK 74119
www.tulsacc.edu

## Oregon

Central Oregon Community College
Bend, OR 97701
www.cocc.edu

Chemeketa Community College
Salem, OR 97309
www.chemek.cc.or.us

Clatsop Community College
Astoria, OR 97103
www.clatsopcc.edu

Linn-Benton Community College
Albany, OR 97321
www.linnbenton.edu

Mount Hood Community College
Gresham, OR 97030
www.mhcc.edu

Portland Community College
Portland, OR 97280
www.pcc.edu

Rogue Community College
Grants Pass, OR 97527
www.roguecc.edu

Southwestern Oregon Community College
Coos Bay, OR 97420
www.socc.edu

Treasure Valley Community College
Ontario, OR 97914
www.tvcc.cc.or.us

## *Pennsylvania*

Butler County Community College
Butler, PA 16003
http://bc3.cc.pa.us

Community College of Allegheny County–Boyce
Monroeville, PA 15146
www.ccac.edu

Community College of Allegheny County–North
Pittsburgh, PA 15237
www.ccac.edu

Community College of Allegheny County–South
West Mifflin, PA 15122
www.ccac.edu

Community College of Beaver County
Monaca, PA 15061
www.ccbc.edu

Harrisburg Area Community College
Harrisburg, PA 17110
www.hacc.edu

Lehigh Carbon Community College
Schnecksville, PA 18078
www.lccc.edu

Westmoreland County Community College
Youngwood, PA 15697
www.wccc-pa.edu

## *South Carolina*

Aiken Technical College
Aiken, SC 29802
www.aik.tec.sc.us

Central Carolina Technical College
Sumter, SC 29150
www.sum.tec.sc.us

Denmark Technical College
Denmark, SC 29042
www.denmarktech.edu

Florence Darlington Technical College
Florence, SC 29501
www.fdtc.edu

Greenville Technical College
Greenville, SC 29606
www.greenvilletech.com

Horry-Georgetown Technical College
Conway, SC 29528
www.hor.tec.sc.us

Piedmont Technical College
Greenwood, SC 29648
www.ptc.edu

Spartanburg Technical College
Spartanburg, SC 29305
www.stcsc.edu

Tri-County Technical College
Pendleton, SC 29670
www.tctc.edu

Trident Technical College
Charleston, SC 29423
www.tridenttech.edu

## *Tennessee*

Cleveland State Community College
Cleveland, TN 37320
www.clscc.cc.tn.us

Jackson State Community College
Jackson, TN 38301
www.jscc.edu

Nashville State Community College
Nashville, TN 37209
www.nscc.edu

Northeast State Technical Community College
Blountville, TN 37617
www.nstcc.cc.tn.us

Walters State Community College
Morristown, TN 37813
www.wscc.cc.tn.us

## *Texas*

Angelina College
Lufkin, TX 75902
www.angelina.cc.tx.us

El Paso Community College
El Paso, TX 79998
www.epcc.edu

Grayson County College
Denison, TX 75020
www.grayson.edu

Houston Community College System
Houston, TX 77270
www.hccs.cc.tx.us

Kilgore College
Kilgore, TX 75662
www.kilgore.edu

Laredo Community College
Laredo, TX 78040
www.laredo.edu

Midland College
Midland, TX 79701
www.midland.edu

Odessa College
Odessa, TX 79762
www.odessa.edu

South Plains College
Levelland, TX 79336
www.southplainscollege.edu

Tarrant County College
Fort Worth, TX 76102
www.tccd.edu

Texas Southmost College
Brownsville, TX 78520
www.utb.edu

## Utah

College of Eastern Utah
Price, UT 84501
www.ceu.edu

Salt Lake Community College
Salt Lake City, UT 84130
www.slcc.edu

## Virginia

Central Virginia Community College
Lynchburg, VA 24502
www.cvcc.vccs.edu

Dabney S. Lancaster Community College
Clifton Forge, VA 24422
www.dl.vccs.edu

John Tyler Community College
Chester, VA 23831
www.jtcc.edu

Lord Fairfax Community College
Middletown, VA 22645
www.lf.vccs.edu

Mountain Empire Community College
Big Stone Gap, VA 24219
www.me.vccs.edu

New River Community College
Dublin, VA 24084
www.nr.edu

Northern Virginia Community College
Annandale, VA 22003
www.nvcc.vccs.edu

Patrick Henry Community College
Martinsville, VA 24112
www.ph.vccs.edu

Southside Virginia Community College
Alberta, VA 23821
www.sv.vccs.edu

Southwest Virginia Community College
Richlands, VA 24641
www.sw.vccs.edu

Thomas Nelson Community College
Hampton, VA 23670
www.tncc.vccs.edu

Tidewater Community College
Portsmouth, VA 23510
www.tcc.vccs.edu

Wytheville Community College
Wytheville, VA 24382
www.wcc.vccs.edu

## Washington

Centralia College
Centralia, WA 98531
www.centralia.ctc.edu

Clark College
Vancouver, WA 98663
www.clark.edu

Columbia Basin Community College
Pasco, WA 99301
www.columbiabasin.edu

Edmonds Community College
Lynnwood, WA 98036
www.edcc.edu

Pierce College
Tacoma, WA 98498
www.pierce.ctc.edu

Skagit Valley College
Mount Vernon, WA 98273
www.skagit.edu

Walla Walla Community College
Walla Walla, WA 99362
www.wwcc.edu/home

## *West Virginia*

West Virginia Northern Community College
Wheeling, WV 26003
www.northern.wvnet.edu

West Virginia University at Parkersburg
Parkersburg, WV 26101
www.wvup.edu

## *Wisconsin*

Black Hawk Technical College
Janesville, WI 53547
www.blackhawk.tec.wi.us

Gateway Technical College
Kenosha, WI 53141
www.gtc.edu

Madison Area Technical College
Madison, WI 53714
http://matcmadison.edu/matc

Northeast Wisconsin Technical College
Green Bay, WI 54307
www.nwtc.tec.wi.us

## *Wyoming*

Casper College
Casper, WY 82601
www.caspercollege.edu

Central Wyoming College
Riverton, WY 82501
www.cwc.edu

Western Wyoming Community College
Rock Springs, WY 82901
www.wwcc.cc.wy.us

# Appendix C

# *Selected Organizations Related to Electronics*

American Electronics Association
5201 Great American Pkwy., Ste. 520
Santa Clara, CA 95054
www.aeanet.org

American Engineering Association
4116 S. Carrier Pkwy.
Grand Prairie, TX 75052
www.aea.org

Armed Forces Communications and Electronics Association
AFCEA Headquarters
4400 Fair Lakes Ct.
Fairfax, VA 22033-3899
www.afcea.org

Association of Communications and Electronics Schools
    International (ACES)
5241 Princess Anne Rd., Ste. 110
Virginia Beach, VA 23462
www.acesinternational.org

Canadian Academy of Engineering
180 Elgin St., Ste. 1100
Ottawa, ON K2P 2K3
www.acad-eng-gen.ca

Canadian Council of Technicians and Technologists
285 McLeod St.
Ottawa, ON K2P 1A1
www.cctt.ca

Canadian Society for Engineering Management
1295 Hwy. 2 E.
Kingston, ON K7L 4V1
www.csem-scgi.ca

Canadian Solar Industries Association
2378 Holly La., Ste. 208
Ottawa, ON K1V 7P1
www.cansia.ca

Electro-Federation Canada
5800 Explorer Dr., Ste. 200
Mississauga, ON L4W 5K9
www.electrofed.com

Electronic Industries Alliance
2500 Wilson Blvd.
Arlington, VA 22201
www.eia.org

Electronic Industries Association
777 E. Eisenhower Pkwy.
Ann Arbor, MI 48108
www.techstreet.com

Electronics Technicians Association, International
5 Depot St.
Greencastle, IN 46135
www.eta-i.org

Institute of Electrical and Electronics Engineers (IEEE)
IEEE Operations Center
445 Hoes La.
Piscataway, NJ 08854-1331
www.ieee.org

IEEE Corporate Office
3 Park Ave., 17th Fl.
New York, NY 10016-5997
www.ieee.org

International Federation of Professional and Technical Engineers
8630 Fenton St.
Silver Spring, MD 20910
www.ifpte.org

International Society of Certified Electronics Technicians
3608 Pershing Ave.
Fort Worth, TX 76107-4527
www.iscet.org

International Union of Electronic, Electrical, Salaried, Machine, and
    Furniture Workers
1126 16th St. NW
Washington, DC 20036
www.iue-cwa.org

National Electronic Service Dealers Association
3608 Pershing Ave.
Fort Worth, TX 76107
www.nesda.com

United States Telephone Association
607 14th NW, Ste. 400
Washington, DC 20005
www.usta.org

# Further Reading

Bennett, Scott. *The Elements of Résumé Style: Essential Rules and Eye-Opening Advice for Writing Résumés and Cover Letters That Work.* New York: AMACOM, 2005.

Eberts, Marjorie, and Margaret Gisler. *Careers for Computer Buffs and Other Technological Types.* Chicago: McGraw-Hill, 2006.

Emko, Tod, and Evan Koblentz. *Vault Guide to Technology Careers.* New York: Vault, Inc., 2005.

Floyd, Thomas L. *Electronics Fundamentals: Circuits, Devices, and Applications.* Upper Saddle River, N.J.: Prentice Hall, 2006.

Garner, Geraldine. *Careers in Engineering.* Chicago: McGraw-Hill, 2002.

Gibilisco, Stan. *Teach Yourself Electricity and Electronics.* Chicago: McGraw-Hill, 2006.

Hughes, Edward. *Hughes Electrical and Electronic Technology.* Upper Saddle River, N.J.: Prentice Hall, 2005.

Khairallah, Michael. *Physical Security Systems Handbook: The Design and Implementation of Electronic Security Systems.* Boston: Butterworth-Heinemann, 2005.

Kleitz, William. *Digital Electronics: A Practical Approach.* Upper Saddle River, N.J.: Prentice Hall, 2004.

*Occupational Outlook Handbook.* Washington, DC: U.S. Department of Labor, 2006.

Paynter, Robert, and Toby Boydell. *Electronics Technology Fundamentals—Electron Flow.* Upper Saddle River, N.J.: Prentice Hall, 2004.

*Résumés for Scientific and Technical Careers.* Chicago: McGraw-Hill, 1999.

Rudman, Jack. *Electronic Technician* (USPS). Syosset, N.Y.: National Learning Corporation, 2006.

Schultz, Mitchel E. *Grob's Basic Electronics.* New York: McGraw-Hill, 2006.

## About the Author

Mark Rowh is a widely published writer as well as an experienced educator in community college and vocational-technical education. He is a vice president at New River Community College in Dublin, Virginia, and has also held administrative positions at Greenville (South Carolina) Technical College and at Bluefield State College and Parkersburg Community College in West Virginia.

Rowh holds a doctorate in vocational and technical education from Clemson University, and he has worked closely with a variety of technical programs in his career as a professional educator.

Rowh's articles on educational and career topics have appeared in a wide range of magazines.